THE MOVING BALANCE SYSTEM...
A NEW TECHNIQUE FOR STOCK & OPTION TRADING

The Moving Balance System…
A New Technique For
Stock & Option Trading

by Humphrey E. D. Lloyd, M. D.

Windsor Books, Brightwaters, N.Y.

Published by Windsor Books
P. O. Box 280
Brightwaters, N. Y., 11718

Manufactured in the United States of America

To my wife, Mary,

To my sons, Aidan, Owen, and David,

To my daughters, Noelle and Genevieve

And in Memory of Breffni.

Acknowledgment

I should like to thank Gerald Appel, editor of *"Systems and Forecasts,"* for permission to reproduce Figure 9. I am also grateful to Robert M. Bleiberg, Editor of *Barron's* [*Dow Jones & Company*] for permission to reproduce the Table on page 60.

It is a pleasure to record the invaluable help given by Joanne DeSantis. A great deal of her work involved deciphering my hieroglyphics. Not only did she do this excellently but, with dispatch, she changed them into beautiful typescript.

Finally, I should like to thank Mr. George A. Nikas for writing the Foreward. He is an expert and I am most honored.

Foreword

Dr. Humphrey E. D. Lloyd has written a book which is extremely informative and timely. His subject matter deals with the most essential ingredients in a successful investment program. He has chosen the "option" which, in theory and actual practice, is the most versatile investment vehicle available to the investing public today, thanks to the development of the CBOE and ASE listed option markets. The "versatile option" allows him to develop numerous strategies based on stock market dynamics without deviating from the all important investment objectives of the investor.

Dr. Lloyd's moving balance indicator (MBI) will assist the investor in meeting Wall Street's greatest and most demanding challenge—timing!

The "MBI" will not only help keep you from buying when you should be selling, but will also allow you to gauge the technical strength or weakness of the market.

Whether you are one of the millions of investors who lost 130 billion dollars of market value in 1974, or were astute enough to profit by the "bear market," unrivaled since the 1930's, you will find Dr. Lloyd's combination of self-disciplined suggestions and creative trading strategies to be an essential investment tool.

The Moving Balance System...A New Technique For Stock & Option Trading is must reading for Wall Street "aficionados"—or the aspiring novice.

George A. Nikas
Vice President - Options Department
Burgess & Leith
Boston, Ma. 02109

UPDATE ON THE MBI

Back in 1983, I updated the MBI originally described in my book, *"The Moving Balance System,"* published by Windsor Books in 1976. This update gave three ways of correcting the markedly increased trading volume since the book was published. These corrections worked well until the October 1987 freefall when, as most people know, the market almost disappeared. The MKDS values which are used as one of the components in the MBI went to levels never even dreamt of so bearish were they, and this seems to be a good time to redesign the MBI and to volume-proof it once and for all. The MBI, therefore, is now redesigned with the three components as follows:

1. The AD figure is exactly as given in the book with a ten-day moving average of the advancing issues divided by the ten-day moving average of the declining issues multiplied by ten.

2. Daily volume figures are worked out as follows: The advancing volume is divided by the total of advancing volume plus declining volume. Ignore any unchanged volume. This figure is multiplied by one hundred to give a percentage and a ten-day moving average of this figure is run. This ten-day moving average is divided by three and becomes the second component of the MBI. The reason for dividing by three is to balance it with the first AD component.

3. Finally, the ten-day moving average of the MKDS is run exactly as described in the book. However, the assigned values have now been changed in order to cope with the highly bearish readings obtained in October.

When I was working on the MBI, the highest I thought the ten-day moving average of the MKDS could ever be expected to reach was 1.85. Remember, the MKDS is a reciprocal indicator and a reading of this level would be highly bearish. October 1987 changed all that and a ten-day moving average reading of 3.95 was attained on October 26. That is the most bearish reading ever, and I hope we don't try and challenge it in the near future. At any rate, the new ten-day moving average assigned values are as follows:

$$0.6 = 12.5 \quad 0.7 = 12.0 \quad 0.8 = 11.5 \quad 0.9 = 11.0 \quad 1.0 = 10.5 \quad \text{etc.}$$

and so on down to 3.1 which is zero and 4 which is -4.5. I am very much hoping we don't get down there again. Notice also that the ten-day moving averages are now rounded off to the nearest decimal point, and that there are no intermediate points as there were previously. For instance, a ten-day moving average of 1.132 is counted as 10, i.e., as 1.1, and a ten-day moving average of 1.151 is counted as 9.5, i.e., a moving average of 1.2. As in the old MBI, the three components are added together, multiplied by two, and rounded off to the nearest whole number. I have done quite a bit of work and thinking about this but I confess I haven't had the time to go back over the years to see what the charts would look like. But, I am pleased to have found a way to have got the volume figure under control. Although I presently have data back only to the beginning of October, it is obvious looking at the data during this time that a new MBI value around 60 is a good support area and a new MBI value over 90 represents resistance remembering, however, that the market may keep on going upwards for awhile as the MBI corrects. (See Page 166 in "The Moving Balance System.")

Humphrey E.D. Lloyd, M.D.

Illustrations

Table Of Contents

Introduction

AN IMPORTANT DISCLAIMER

This book describes a system, the Moving Balance System; based on an indicator, the Moving Balance Indicator. This indicator is derived from the action of all the stocks traded on the New York Stock Exchange, the Big Board. These stocks really are, to a very large extent, "the market."

No one can predict (and I certainly do not claim that I can predict) how "the market" will behave in the future. But I believe in the strong possibility that it will, in the future, behave in a way that is more or less related to the pattern of its behavior in the near past. If it does so, then the system I describe will work.

However, if "the market" decides to behave in some completely new and different way, then it is clear that no system based on its previous behavior can be expected to stand much of a chance. But if the swings from excessive investor optimism (overbought) to excessive investor pessimism (oversold) continue, "the market," as I have come to know it, will continue. What follows is designed to give the market player an edge. The market is always quick to "call one a liar"—no matter how knowledgeable that someone may be. But I believe that it is far better to have a system that provides a logical basis for action (even if the market, acting "illogically," fails to behave as expected) than not to have a system at all. The system I describe can *not* pick the exact reversal points. But then no system that I know of can. As one respected investment advisor said at a seminar I attended recently, "All I want to do is get you in the ball park." It is my hope that not only will the Moving Balance System get you into the ball park, but that it will also help you to set up your own plays once you are there.

SOME WORDS OF ENCOURAGEMENT

It is apparent that a stopped clock is correct twice-a-day. The idea behind this book is that the above performance can be improved upon.

This book falls naturally into two parts. The first describes the search for a reliable market indicator; the second the application of a system, based on this indicator, to stock and option trading. There is nothing difficult about calculating the Moving Balance Indicator, and immediate use can be made of this indicator for timing stock purchases and sales as soon as the relevant data are collected and the underlying concepts understood.

However, the Moving Balance System is essentially a *relatively short-term* trading system. Techniques for hedging and spread trading in options are given and various formulae are presented for working out break-even points. I have not assumed any previous option trading experience or indeed any specialized market knowledge on the reader's part. Though the second part looks complicated, actually it is not. I suggest that you read the whole book through quickly once in order to get a feel for the moving balance *concept*. Individual chapters can be studied more carefully. The chapter on spread trading should be examined in depth by anyone seriously considering option trading.

The advantage of the Moving Balance Indicator is that it provides an unemotional way of judging the state of the market. As you work with it you will develop a feeling of confidence and self-reliance, and you will find that this desirable state of affairs will not normally require more than two hour's work a week and sometimes not as much. I wish you every success.

CHAPTER 1

LEARN A LITTLE ABOUT ME AND AS MUCH AS POSSIBLE ABOUT YOURSELF

Chapter 1

Learn A Little About Me And
As Much As Possible About Yourself

"The fault, dear Brutus, is not in our stars, but in ourselves that we are underlings."

W. Shakespeare, Julius Caesar.

For many people, "playing the stock market" is a form of disguised—sometimes only partially disguised—self-punishment and as such is akin to other activities capable of profound internal disruption, such as golf and chess. Imagine for a moment the turmoil produced inside a golfer, any golfer, after missing a crucial short putt or the terrible feeling of doom after committing a blunder in chess. Bobby Fischer, the greatest chess player who ever lived, made an almost unbelievable blunder in game one for the 1971 world championship against Boris Spassky at Reykjavik. A mistake in playing the market is at any rate not public, but it hurts greatly just the same.

I was born under the sign of Leo to a Leo mother and a Leo father. This set of givens did not mean anything to me at the time but I was not far into childhood before I detected an attitude in myself that I have subsequently learned is typically Leo—namely "I can do anything better than anyone else—(or, at worst, at least as well)." The fault may not be in my stars, but it is essential to know their influence, if one is truly to know oneself. And I firmly believe that success in any endeavor, but *particularly in the stock market,* can only be achieved by true self-knowledge.

19

At any rate, I chose medicine as a career and I specialize in pathology—laboratory medicine. One of my important responsibilities is the microscopic diagnosis of tissues removed by surgeons. This requires me to be substantially correct close to 100% of the time; not necessarily in the very fine details but in the broad sweep of diagnosis. If I say a mass is malignant, the surgeon has to take my word for it and treat the patient for malignancy. If I am wrong, so, automatically, is he. Under these circumstances, and particularly considering the way surgeons are, I cannot afford to make mistakes. So, I have had to develop a high degree of confidence in my decisions.

This last sentence is a real clue to self-understanding. It says in effect (1) I want to be correct, (2) I cannot stand uncertainty. It also implies that I do not find decision making particularly difficult—just that I want to be correct. And other physicians who are not pathologists, nevertheless have to be correct in a high percentage of their professional decisions. It is just this degree of success of their non-market activities that causes the downfall and haphazard, if not downright disastrous, performance of many physicians in the market place. A man who is used to being substantially correct has a hard time admitting to himself, or to anyone else, that he is wrong. It is easier to think in terms of "only a paper loss" with ultimate recovery, vindication and profit.

My own experience in the market is probably not unusual. In 1967, having five hundred dollars to play with, I decided to put it to work and on a friend's advice bought ten shares of Hewlett-Packard at forty-two. I sold out in 1968 at eighty-six, wondering how anything could be so easy. Immediately, I bought twenty shares of LTV Electro-systems, around forty, (on the advice of the same friend). In 1970, I bailed out in disgust at ten. Between 1970 and 1972, I managed to lose, by one means or another, and all of them apparently logical, about ten thousand dollars in actual money, and at least another five thousand dollars "on paper."

On December 25, 1972, I decided to give myself a present. I vowed to give the market, and my interaction with the market, my best effort to see if by so doing I could learn to be successful. If I failed, I was going to get out and stay out. I was lucky at this time to run across a book by Larry Williams, *The Secret Of Selecting Stocks For Immediate And Substantial Gains*. This book gave me some useful ideas that played an important part in the evolution of the system I am going to describe. However, the system is mine. It is based on the idea that when the market becomes unbalanced forces *inside itself* will move to restore the balance. It is, for this reason, called the Moving Balance System. I wrote this book for three reasons:

1) I would like my readers to be aware of my mistakes and hopefully to profit from them by avoiding similar mistakes. I am not trying to prevent them from making mistakes entirely, as the making of mistakes is part of the learning process. But, what I would like to prevent, if I can, is the totally unnecessary loss of significant amounts of money due to the kind of mistakes that I made in the past.

2) I would also like to suggest a system to those who are presently not satisfied with their performance in the market and who need an uncomplicated but relatively scientific approach to the market. In this regard, many books on the stock market seem to be so full of advice on what *not* to do—for example, William X. Scheinman's book, *Why Investors Are Mostly Wrong Most of The Time*—that they manage to avoid giving any concrete help on how to tackle the market in the future. I would like this to be a practical book and I wish to record what I have learned from the work I did. The figures are accurate and should prove to be valuable on their own.

3) I would like to make some money for myself while the market is making some for me.

As far as possible, I wish to avoid sounding as though I am giving advice because that is not what I want to do. What I want to do is to describe a system that can be shown to have worked in the past. The disclaimer, already formulated, must be made against assuming that similar results can be achieved in the future. But the built-in safety features of the system act as a significant protection against substantial loss. I have confidence in my system and believe that the future results can be as good or better. Earlier, I have claimed that only two hour's work a week are necessary. This is true after some work in depth has been done on your own personality to assess your volatility. Knowing your volatility index is crucial. I believe that there are basically three levels of volatility which have a bearing on stock market success, and I am going to ask you to answer the following questionnaire to find out for yourself into which category you fall.

Questionnaire

1) The planets were in a particular position in the heavens at the exact time and place of your birth. Do you believe that this:
    (a) Could have a profound effect on your personality.
    (b) Could not possibly be of any real significance.
    (c) May be in some part responsible for the person you are now.

2) Which would you prefer:
    (a) A 1 in 1 chance of making $100.
    (b) A 1 in 10 chance of making $1000.
    (c) A 1 in 100 chance of making $10,000.

3) If something does not turn out properly do you:
    (a) Find yourself full of ready made excuses.
    (b) Try to analyze exactly what went wrong.
    (c) Ignore the whole thing.

4) Do you find decision making:
    (a) Relatively easy most of the time.
    (b) Noticeably difficult.
    (c) Easy.

5) Which would you prefer for a special occasion:
    (a) An American wine you knew well.
    (b) An expensive imported wine you did not know at all.
    (c) A choice of wines.

6) Non-fathers should try it anyway.
  If your teenage daughter told you she was pregnant would you:
    (a) Demand to know the boy's name.
    (b) Ask her if she had taken a confirmatory pregnancy test.
    (c) Tell her it's her problem.

7) Is your handwriting:
    (a) Reasonably legible and quite fast.
    (b) Slow and beautifully legible.
    (c) Fast (and dreadful).

8) When you to go a party does your personality:
   (a) Remain pretty much the same.
   (b) Expand favorably.
   (c) Change markedly.

9) If someone insults you, do you:
   (a) Ignore him but brood for weeks.
   (b) Laugh at him.
   (c) Lash back at him.

10) How would you rate your own chances of being successful in the market?
   (a) 90%
   (b) 50%
   (c) 20%

11) At the end of the month (or similar budget period), have you:
   (a) Always got some money remaining.
   (b) Got a pile of bills left over to be paid next month.
   (c) Balanced your budget most of the time.

12) If you won $100,000 in a lottery would you:
   (a) Put it in a Savings Bank until you had worked out an investment plan.
   (b) Turn it over to an investment counselor.
   (c) Know immediately how you would invest it.

13) When you are asked to recall a poem you knew in childhood, do you find:
   (a) You can remember it perfectly.
   (b) You can remember a good deal of it but cannot really get it all together.
   (c) You really cannot remember much about it.

14) If someone offers you a basket of wild mushrooms assuring you they are edible, do you:
   (a) Decline the offer on the grounds you know nothing about wild mushrooms.
   (b) Believe him and treat them like cultivated mushrooms.
   (c) Accept and try just a few mushrooms.

15) On Sundays, do you:

    (a) Take it easy and let the world come to you.

    (b) Feel uneasy unless you are doing something.

    (c) Usually have something planned.

16) When presented with a difficult problem do you:

    (a) Try and get someone else to solve it.

    (b) Give it the old college try but abandon it if you cannot solve it.

    (c) Stick with it until it is solved.

17) The unmarried should give this one a whirl also.

Is your wife of noticeably different temperament from the girls you dated when single?

    (a) Yes.

    (b) No.

    (c) No reply to (a) or (b) because of the variety of girls dated.

18) If you had to choose your profession or job over again would you:

    (a) Go the same route.

    (b) Try something different.

    (c) Make sure you were more successful in your present job by doing things differently.

19) Are your favorite investment vehicles:

    (a) High yielding securities.

    (b) Mutual funds.

    (c) Glamour stocks.

    (d) None of these.

20) If you were told that you had to get out of the market and stay out would you be:

    (a) Genuinely disappointed.

    (b) Indifferent.

    (c) Secretly pleased.

In the appendix, the three levels of the Volatility Index are plotted. It is essential to know your own level of volatility because *knowing your Volatility Index is an integral part of the Moving Balance System.*

CHAPTER 2

THE VOLATILITY INDEX

Chapter 2

The Volatility Index

There are about 25 million people in the market—the actual number is unimportant. Obviously, a group this size includes every conceivable variety of approach to life, love, and the management of one's financial affairs. I find it entirely credible that for a large number of these people the real reason they are there is *not* primarily to make money but for the prestige and fascination of being there.

"Tis better to have loved and lost, than never to have loved at all."
Alfred, Lord Tennyson

The market is excitement and to be there at all implies discretionary income. There are not many men, after all, who can look you squarely in the eye and say, without a trace of an apology, "I put my money into a Savings Bank at 5½%."

The idea behind the Volatility Index is to make you aware of the strength of your emotions. Emotions may be fine in the world outside, but to be in any way governed by them in the market is disastrous. At this point, I hope you know your Volatility Index. If it is high, as mine is, you have my sympathy as you will need all the protection you can get in your interaction with the market. The system—The Moving Balance System—will give you just such protection. Forgive me if I go slowly, but this early assessment of volatility is really very important. Perhaps it will help if I give you my idea of the prototypes of each degree of volatility. I admit to a certain exaggeration, but if I can get across the fact that one's own emotional volatility is to a very large extent responsible for any lack of success, such exaggeration is permissible.

High Volatility Index (Volatility Index over 45)

Prototype: Richard I [the Lionhearted] King of England 1189 - 1199

Richard, with Barbarossa and Philip II of France, led the third crusade against the infidel. The trouble with men like Richard is that they are always rushing off on emotional enterprises. What could be more emotional than a crusade, after all? A new idea—a new enthusiasm, my God, this is the life. One of the reasons the third crusade was not more successful (ignoring the mid-east Montezuma's revenge) was that Richard was always wanting to try out new weapons and new tactics without consulting with the other leaders. And while he was gallivanting around being a crusader, he totally ignored his responsibilities to his people and kingdom leaving them to the mercy of his brother John. And as anyone who saw Errol Flynn as Robin Hood knows, John was not a nice man at all. Men like Richard have a hell of a time admitting to themselves that they are barking up the wrong tree. They would much rather try barking louder than go find the correct tree. In love they act first and ask questions afterwards; questions such as "By the way, what did you say your name was?"

Medium Volatility Index (Volatility Index between 30 and 45)

Prototype: James Bond 007

Ian Fleming idealized the man of medium volatility and Sean Connery, in the good days, did a rather marvelous job of making 007 credible. The most terrific characteristic such men have is a *resistance to panic*. The man of high volatility index may appear outwardly calm in a dangerous situation but inwardly his emotions are all over the lot, whereas the man of medium volatility index is pleasantly stimulated by danger. Such men actually are rare. Unfortunately, what happens to a man of medium volatility index—if he is unaccustomed to danger—is that, when confronted by it, he reacts uncharacteristically. His volatility index rises (the process is not under his control) and he responds emotionally like a man of high volatility index. Just recall for a moment some of the situations James Bond encountered. In real life, he might indeed have acted differently, but if confronted with a situation like the laser beam in "Goldfinger" how do you think you would have reacted? I know that I would not have been able to think of "Operation Grandslam," the one expression that made Goldfinger turn off the damned beam. And, not to get too discouraging, being in the market *without a system* feels not unlike being strapped to a table a la Bond waiting for the laser.

Low Volatility Index (Volatility Index below 30)

Prototype: Mr. Spock First Officer of the U.S.S. Enterprise in "Startrek"

Mr. Spock is, of course, an exaggeration on his own. There are few people, men or women, who are as truly unemotional as Spock, who deal only in and with logic. He has the advantage, of course, of being half-Vulcan. He is, however, a most useful type to have in one's mind as an ideal decision maker for opening transactions in the market, but not for closing transactions. The closer one can approach pure logic the better and clearer one's decisions will be. The only trouble is that the market itself is not logical and the Spocks of this world do not move fast enough when illogicality occurs.

Let us imagine a highly unlikely situation for a moment, but one with its amusements. Let us suppose that each of our three prototypes has by some curious circumstance become owner of 100 shares of a stock destined for great things—Futurex. Richard, who must now be moved to the Twentieth Century, becomes terrifically enthusiastic about the stock. He talks about it, eats with it, and his head is full of it as he tries to get to sleep. Indeed, the thought of the terrific future possiblities actually keeps him awake. Sure enough, the stock takes off and keeps on going until his capital has increased 7 fold. At this point a correction occurs; Richard reacts emotionally, suffers, panics and liquidates his position. His profit is still 5 times his original investment and he lets everyone know how smart he has been. He promptly puts all his winnings onto a dark horse, one which, it turns out, can only run backwards.

James Bond, on the other hand, realizing that a correction was inevitable and that the whole market is in an intermediate oversold condition, buys more. The stock again takes off, splitting and then splitting again. James stays on top of the situation. He sells out close to the all-time high. His original investment is returned almost 200 fold. He remarks casually one day to his barber, "I'm glad I got out of Futurex when I did. Have you seen what's happened to it lately?" Barber: "Gee, I have a guy who used to talk about that stock all the time. But he made so much dough in it he got out with his profit. He's now into some real hot stock called Magic-Mem. The outfit is developing a machine to do away with computer cards or something like that." James: "How's it doing?" Barber: "Well, not too well right now, I guess, but this guy's got real flair and I'm thinking of buying some myself!"

Spock never talks about his investments. He bought Futurex at $1.00 a share. He is not moved when his shares rise in value on an adjusted basis to $200.00 per share. He does nothing when the stock tumbles drastically. If asked he will say, "I got them for $1.00 a share. It is logical to assume that since they have been worth as much as $200.00 per share recently, they will ultimately be worth more than that."

CHAPTER 3

ANALYZING PAST MISTAKES

Chapter 3

Analyzing Past Mistakes

"Those who do not remember the past are condemned to relive it."
George Santayana

At this point you know my Volatility index is high, and hopefully you know your own level.

Before you read what is to follow, it will prove valuable for you to jot down as objectively as possible all the mistakes you have made in the past in the market and then compare them with my list. It is important to state somewhere that I do not consider myself to be any kind of a market expert. This may be a funny place to put that statement, right in front of my list of ferocious mistakes, but although I think I know how to handle myself in the market, this does not mean that I learned to do so by studying the market exclusively. I had to study the market, of course, but one of the realizations that evolved from the study was that my lack of market knowledge was only partially responsible for my failure. For instance, it finally came to me one night while sipping a brandy after dinner that deep down—right down at the center—I expected that my presence in a particular stock would have a noticeable effect on that stock's performance. This attitude took quite a bit of unearthing and because it is basically so egotistical and conceited I had to have a few passes at it before I allowed myself to realize that my subconscious expected some kind of message to go out over the wires; something like "Lloyd's in for 50 shares. He must know something—let's buy."

Of course, holding such an attitude, I kept on getting creamed. *I* knew I was right; all the other guys were wrong. Well, that attitude was a mistake of such magnitude that I am not going to dwell on it further. Instead will follow a list of the mistakes I made which more closely relate to lack of market savvy.

1) Not knowing the short and intermediate term trends of the market; in fact, for years, not even realizing that such trends existed. All I knew was that the market went down from time to time when the overall trend was up or vice versa.

2) Because of the failure to realize that short term trends fluctuate around long term trends, I bought at tops and sold at bottoms with alarming precision. Also, I managed to be wrong at the major turning points.

3) Jumping into a situation on a hot tip with both feet without waiting to test the water, or indeed to find out if there was any water there at all.

4) Allowing emotions to alter my plans.

5) Failure to cut losses. This, in the long run, was the most costly, and the ability to cut losses proved to be the most difficult attitude to acquire.

6) Failure to sell short (see Chapter 11) because it was "risky." The only way to make money overall in the bear market is to be heavily on the short side or out altogether. Ask anyone who stayed long from the January '73 top to early October of '74.

7) Not being in tune with my broker. In 1970, I had a smart broker. At least, he told me he was smart and anyway, he had to be smarter than I was because he invested all the time. He made me feel uncomfortable and incompetent, so to test him, I sent him twenty-five hundred dollars to see what he could do. He bought me a hundred shares of United Founders Life at fifteen and a hundred-fifty warrants of the Mortgage Trust of America at six and a quarter. United Founders Life went straight down. I got out at four (how could I have gone on listening to his talk of recovery all that time??). The stock dropped out of the OTC lists and I think the company must have gone bankrupt. The Mortgage Trust of America warrants fell to three and got back to five where I insisted on bailing out. They went briefly to nine before falling from there to an eighth bid the last time I

looked. This could be called listening to the wrong broker.

8) Equally bad is not listening to the right broker. Needless to say, I left the broker described and found someone I could work with. It is essential to realize that the client and his broker are a team. When something doesn't look right to the man on the spot, his word should be heeded. One example of that— I had read a book on point and figure charting and General Motors had just given what I thought was a classical sell signal. So eager to try my luck and not realizing that the whole market was deeply oversold, I called him up to buy me a put on G.M. His advice was as follows, "I certainly wouldn't do it now at these levels; if you really must buy one, let it rally to its resistance line." I went ahead anyway and lost five-hundred dollars just like that. But think of the amount of fine wine five-hundred dollars would buy, or for that matter, five star cognac. Note also that I would have been creamed if instead of the put (see Chapter 12), I had shorted the stock.

9) Not using stops.

10) Using stops incorrectly. Stops are a vital protection against serious mistakes when an unhedged position is taken but they should be used only in conjunction with short term market trends which will be described later. Otherwise, the possibilities of getting stopped out are great; and to be stopped out of a position, which ultimately would have turned out to be very profitable, is hopelessly frustrating.

11) Reading too many books and trying too many systems without having a feel for what I was doing. I read, for example, a book by J. M. Hurst called, *The Profit Magic Of Stock Transaction Timing.* I think it is probably a very good book. It is certainly complicated and seems very scientific. At any rate, I had been following Syntex on time cycles as advised, drawing tighter and tighter trend lines. When Syntex broke its most recent trend line, I confidently went ahead and put my order in with a stop two points below. However, at that time, I did not realize the difference between a stop limit order on the American Exchange and a stop loss on the Big Board. When the stocks slid ten points on me, just like that, I wasn't worried as I thought I had been stopped out. But to my horror, I found the stock hadn't traded at my stock limit and I was still in there with a thousand dollars loss, which I took. The stock ran up subsequently to almost double my

original price. I suppose I was just a little bit off in my timing of the cycles but I really don't know any more vexing experience than to be almost right; lose; and then see the stock make new highs on each succeeding day.

12) Expecting the market to work for me when I wasn't really prepared to work for it.

Things are different now that I have devised my own Moving Balance System. The system is simple and reliable. It requires work every trading day—rain or shine. Under certain circumstances this may mean taking your notebooks on vacation with you in order not to miss an important market turn. If you are, however, fully invested in a hedged or spread position you can take your vacation with equanimity. You are then only faced with the problem of getting the records up-to-date when you return. This means going back over all the daily and weekly statistics for the days of your vacation. Sorry about that, but since each day does not require more than a few minutes work as far as the pure statistics are concerned the task is not very burdensome—just essential.

The Moving Balance System requires no more than ten minutes work a day; about 2 or 3 minutes, at most, for calculating the Moving Balance Indicator and the other seven or eight for reviewing the portfolio and working out some possible plays. Since the market is open five days a week this is only 50 minutes work. About an hour's work is required on weekends to keep up with the option scene and for thinking and planning. You can, in other words, stay in tune with the market on two hour's work a week. It is unnecessary to try and determine what effect individual pieces of good news or bad news will have on the market. The market itself will let you know in due course. With the Moving Balance System you can be prepared, if you so desire, for anything and everything up to and including catastrophic market collapse. Perhaps the most important thing to be learned is that the curious creature, "the market," owes you nothing, and that without some kind of logical approach to decision making, (unless you have real flair), you can't expect to be correct much more frequently than the stopped clock—and that's a terrible batting average.

CHAPTER 4

HOW THE SYSTEM DEVELOPED

Chapter 4

How The System Developed

My interest in the market goes back to 1967. I have read over the years a number of books, without ever being able to find a consistent approach to the market. As I have said, I decided in December 1972 to give the market my best effort. What evolved is my Moving Balance System. Its evolution was complex because several minor factors and two major factors were at work.

Factor 1—The Buy-Sell Index (B-S Index)*

For the first six months of 1973 I devoted a great deal of my spare time to market indicators. This meant going back through past issues of Barron's for 1972 to get a base. I would stay up nights and go to bed with my brain reeling and eyes bleary. Incidentally, looking up past action, while necessary, is also very tedious work. Larry William's book, *The Secret Of Selecting Stocks For Immediate And Substantial Gains,* gave me several indicators to work out. Not long after I had started on such indicators as Will-go, specialist vs. odd-lot short selling, municipal bond yield, etc., Gerald Appel's marvelous book, *Winning Market Systems,* was published. This gave me many more indicators to follow: such as Worden's Tick Volume System, speed resistance lines, stock

---

*This abbreviation, and others used in this book in text or formulae, are defined and explained in the *Glossary & Formulae* sections at the end of the book.

oscillators, etc.

Well, in spite of collecting a great deal of information, I still could not find a system that suited me. Incidentally, it became rather obvious to me early on that I had to have ''a system'' if I wished to achieve any consistency of approach to market decisions.

In March 1973, I began to notice a most interesting fact about two of the indicators I had been following. Larry Williams pointed out in his book that the marketplace on any day is really a battle between buyers and sellers and that the market generally, as well as individual stocks, could be subjected to analysis of buyers vs. sellers.

Buying Pressure he defined as the force that moves stock prices upward. Obviously, any movement up from the previous day's close to the high of the following day is buying pressure and so is any movement up from the low of the day to the close of the day. Let us take an example from those halcyon days when the Dow was over 1000 (remember them?). On Dec. 11, 1972 the Dow closed at 1036.3. On the following day, Dec. 12th, the figures for the action of the Dow were:

Dec. 12th	High	1042.4
	Low	1029.7
	Close	1033.2

Buying pressure then could be derived as follows:

a. High of Dec. 12   1042.4
   Less close of Dec. 11   1036.3
   _____
                                 6.1

b. Close of Dec. 12   1033.2
   Less low of Dec. 12   1029.7
   _____
                                 3.5

i.e., buying pressure had moved the closing price on Dec. 11 *up* 6.1 points to the high of Dec. 12 and had also moved the low of Dec. 12 *up* 3.5 points to the close of Dec. 12. Total buying pressure = 6.1 + 3.5 = *9.6 points.*

Selling Pressure he defined as the force that moves stock prices downwards. The same figures are used as follows. The close of Dec. 11 to *low* of Dec. 12th is obviously selling pressure and so is the difference between the high of Dec. 12th and the close of Dec. 12th. Selling pressure, therefore, is derived as follows:

c. Close of Dec. 11th   1036.3
    Less low of Dec. 12th   <u>1029.7</u>
                        6.6

d. High of Dec. 12th   1042.4
    Less close of Dec. 12th   <u>1033.2</u>
                        9.2

Total selling pressure 6.6 + 9.2 = *15.8* points. Obviously, the total buying pressure plus the total selling pressure = 9.6 + 15.8 points = *25.4 points*

% buying pressure therefore = 9.6/25.4 x 100% = 38%

% selling pressure therefore = 15.8/25.4 x 100% = 62%

i.e. 38% were "buyers," 62% were "sellers." Please note two things—

(1) If a negative figure would be given in working out any of the buying and selling figures—for example, if the high of Dec. 12th never made it to the close of Dec. 11th—count this as zero (*not as a negative*].

(2) Obviously, once the buying pressure has been calculated, selling pressure is equal to 100 minus the buying pressure. It is unnecessary to compute it by division.

Well, so far so good. I had been interested in trying to define for myself "overbought" (too many buyers) and "oversold" (too many sellers), as I had begun to realize that the market is always in motion somewhere between *the extremes of overbought and oversold.* This was a valuable clue. There must be, therefore, an area somewhere, on a % buying-pressure scale, that is "overbought" and an area below this that is "oversold." (Figure 1)

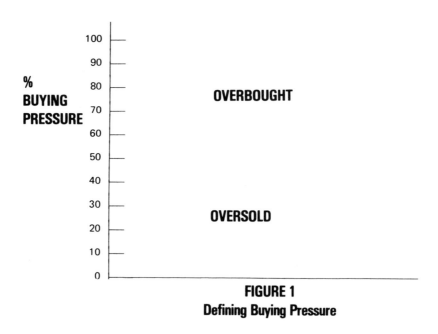

FIGURE 1
Defining Buying Pressure

It would be very useful if the lines of demarcation could be defined with reasonable accuracy as I had also begun to realize that once the market is in one or another of these territories, forces are produced that cause it to move to correct the situation. It never stays *permanently* overbought or oversold. There is indeed a kind of moving balance!

Obviously, the market never gets so overbought that for any period of time there are 100% buyers and no sellers, and similarly it also never gets so oversold that there are no buyers and 100% sellers. Now all we have to discover is that period of time that will give us the most useful frame of reference. It should not be so short that the figures are jumping all over the place; because although this may appear to be the way the market moves to a casual observer, actually the movement is a flow up or down but a definite *flow* in one direction—and this flow necessitates a *reversal point* to move in the opposite direction. The time frame, on the other hand, should not be of such length that significant short term moves are lost.

Therefore, I experimented with the following time frames:

a) 5 days
b) 10 days
c) 20 days

d) 10 weeks
e) 20 weeks

These were picked arbitrarily but I was aware, of course, that both the 10-day time frame and 10 week time frame have been extensively used and studied in terms of market activity, and that the others had also been studied out to a lesser extent. OK—so what is a time frame? It is simply a device for studying a series of values. Consider the following series of days and point a *10 day time frame* at it, say at days 5 thru 14.

```
Days          1 2 3 4 5 6 7 8 9 10 11 12 13 14 15 16 17 18 19 20
                      ↑                      ↑
10 day time frame  1 2 3 4 5   6   7   8   9  10
```

Now imagine that someone takes hold of the top line and pulls it one day to the left. On the time frame below, day 1 now lines up opposite day 6 and runs thru to day 15. Each day the days move one day to the left—the time frame stays still. If you add up the values for *anything that you wish to study* for any group of 10 days, such as days 5 thru 14, you will have a *10 day total*. If you now divide this value by 10 you will have a *10 day average* and if you compute the 10 day averages as each group of 10 days (5-14, 6-15, 7-16, etc.) moves in front of the time frame you will have a *ten day moving average*. Notice it will relate to the *last* day in the series (see later).

For instance, although Larry Williams did not suggest it, I ran 10 day moving averages of the % buying pressure derived in the fashion we have just discussed. Let us take the values for a group of 20 days as follows:

Days	1	2	3	4	5	6	7	8	9	10	11	12	13	14	15	16	17	18	19	20
% Buying Pressure	26	35	40	55	26	47	82	86	59	15	31	69	64	31	42	14	34	35	79	30

Let us now point the time frame at days 1 thru 10, turning it upright as we do so. The 10 day total will be 471—the 10 day average 47.1.

Time Frame	Moving Avg. days	Day	% Buying Pressure					Ten Day Totals	Ten Day Moving Avg. % Buying Pressure
	1	1	26						
	2	2	35						
	3	3	40						
	4	4	55						
	5	5	26						
	6	6	47						
	7	7	82						
	8	8	86						
	9	9	59						
	10	10	15					= 471	47.1
	1	11	31	+	31	–	26	= 476	47.6
	2	12	69	+	69	–	35	= 510	51.0
	3	13	64	+	64	–	40	= 534	53.4
	4	14	31	+	31	–	55	= 510	51.0
	5	15	42	+	42	–	26	= 526	52.6
	6	16	14	+	14	–	47	= 493	49.3
	7	17	34	+	34	–	82	= 445	44.5
	8	18	35	+	35	–	86	= 394	39.4
	9	19	79	+	79	–	59	= 414	41.4
	10	20	30	+	30	–	15	= 429	42.9

The ten day moving average is calculated as follows: On day 11, 31 is added to the 10 day total and 26 subtracted—that is, the time frame now lines up opposite days 2 thru 11. Notice the column on the far left, headed moving average days. Day 11 is the 10 day moving average, new day 1. The cycle repeats every 10 days—only days when the market was open being counted. The value on the new day 1 = *31* replaces that of the old day 1 = *26*. The new 10 day total is now 476 and the 10 day moving average is 47.6. The other days are treated similarly and the 10 day moving average takes shape. Since the middle nine days are common to both the old and new values it is not necessary actually to derive a total from each 10 day time frame. It is absolutely accurate to drop day 1 and add day 11. And the simplest way of doing this, if you do not own an adding machine, is to take one-tenth of the difference and apply it directly to the previous day's moving average. In the table the moving average on day 18 was 39.4. On day 19 the buying pressure was 79% while that on day 9 was 59% (10 days previously), therefore, 79 – 59 = 20; divide by 10 = 2.0. This figure can now be *added* directly to the previous 10 day moving average—i.e., 39.4 + 2.0 = 41.4. If the buying pressure on day 9 was *greater* than on day 19 the difference, divided by 10, would obviously be *subtracted.*

I have spent some time explaining this because moving averages, and particularly 10 day moving averages, are an integral part of my Moving Balance System. Incidentally, if you want to run a 20 day moving average, the easiest way to do so is to apply 1/20 x the difference between days 21 and 1 to the 20 day moving average just as you applied 1/10 x the difference (in the example above) to the 10 day moving average. Well, to return to Larry Williams and his concept of buying vs. selling pressure, I ran 10 and 20 day moving averages of % buying pressure. Since overbought territory, as we have shown, is going to be less than 100% buying pressure and oversold greater than 0% buying pressure, maybe I could derive an index telling me where we were. Let's say, for instance, that the 10 day moving average of the % buying pressure was, on any particular day, 52.2%, i.e., over the previous 10 days on a moving average basis, 52.2% of people were "buyers." This has to mean that 100 - 52.2% = 47.8% were "sellers." Now we can get a Buy/Sell Index (or B/S Index) as follows:

B/S Index = (52.2/47.8) = 1.09. Since I would consider a market with 70% buyers, 30% sellers overbought and one with 30% buyers and 70% sellers oversold—could I use this B/S Index in any useful way? First the B/S Index in overbought territory would be:

$$\frac{70\% \text{ B (buyers)}}{30\% \text{ S (sellers)}} = 2.33 \qquad \text{Index B/S} = 2.33$$

and in oversold territory:

$$\frac{30\% \text{ B (buyers)}}{70\% \text{ S (sellers)}} = 0.43 \qquad \text{Index B/S} = 0.43$$

How did the indicator that I derived from Larry Williams' formula actually stack up in practice? (Affidavit—I have my original notes picking those 70/30 and 30/70 figures before I actually ran the B/S Index out). The results were rather spooky. The highest B/S reading I obtained in 1973 was *2.01.* This was on Jan. 9th, when the market closed at 1047.1 (high of the day was 1053.1. The absolute high of the year 1067.2 was made two days later on Jan. 11th). The lowest reading for 1973 was 0.49 on Aug. 21st, when the Dow closed at 857.8. The following day a low of 845.5 was made before the market took off on a sharp rally of about *150 points*. Was I onto something or was this coincidence?

Well, the interesting fact that I had begun to notice, and mentioned earlier, was that the Advance/Decline Index (A/D Index) derived from the 10 day moving averages of advancing and declining issues moved in remarkable unison with the Buy/Sell Index. The Advance/Decline Index was derived as described below.

On the Big Board, on any given market day a certain number of issues advance and a certain number of issues decline (the unchanged issues are ignored). The 10 day moving average (10 day M.A.) of the issues that advanced is calculated. For example, on any given day the 10 day moving average might be 520.7—meaning that in the past 10 days a *total* of 5207 issues advanced. On this same day the 10 day moving average of the declining issues might be 858.1—meaning that in the past 10 days a *total* of 8581 issues declined. (The figures are for illustration, but actually occurred). The Advance/Decline (A/D) Index is derived as follows:

$$\text{A/D Index} = \frac{\text{10 day M.A. Adv. issues}}{\text{10 day M.A. Decl. issues}} = \frac{520.7}{858.1} = 0.61$$

This index has much the same range as the B/S Index, although the high side is a little lower. *But the values are very similar and move in unison.* The B/S Index, remember, is derived *only* from the action of the Dow, whereas the A/D Index is derived from the total number of issues traded on the Big Board (around 1800 a day are usually traded).

Let me give you some comparisons. On September 6, 1973 the Buy/Sell Index topped out with a high of 1.85, the Advance/Decline Index topped out *the very same day* with a high of 1.70. On December 13th the Buy/Sell Index bottomed out with a reading of *0.71* and the Advance/Decline Index the same day with a reading of *0.61*. Indeed, in the whole of 1973 the longest gap between reversal points was 7 days and they always moved in unison. I don't know if anyone has ever done anything like this before, but for my money this proves to me what a marvelous indicator the Dow really is. Now when I hear someone knocking it; saying that it only tells you what 30 stocks are doing, and not what the other hundreds are doing, I have to smile to myself.

We will return to the Advance/Decline Index again when describing the Moving Balance System in detail. In the meantime, we must move on to the second factor in the evolution of the system.

Factor 2—Warrants and Hedging

I have recorded one brief initial success in the market. I had another success, the significance of which only became apparent to me when I analyzed my failures. In 1970 I read a book, *Beat the Market,* by Thorp and Kassouf. This book dealt with warrant hedging and, rather to my surprise, I understood it. In fact, I developed something of a feel for warrant hedging, but the system never really turned me on, as one had to wait several years for the hedge to pan out.

A *warrant* is a negotiable security traded on a main stock exchange, usually the American Exchange, though some, like the AT&T warrants, are traded on the Big Board. They are issued by a corporation (as a way of raising money) and have very specific terms. What the corporation at the time of the issue of the warrant is saying in effect is: "You give us x dollars and we will, *at any time* up to the expiration date (E.D.) of the warrant, exchange it for y number of shares (usually one) of common stock at the exchange price z dollars, the Exercise Price (E.P.). If you buy a warrant for 3 at an Exercise Price of 20 and the stock at expiration date is 100, you acquire the stock for 20 and you make $100 - 20 - 3$ (the warrant price paid) $= 77$ points. $77/3 \times 100 = 2567\%$ profit. If you buy the warrant from the corporation when issued, you pay x dollars fixed by the corporation, but soon after issue warrants usually become negotiable securities and are traded just like common stock on one of the major exchanges. However, the warrant holder is *not* a shareholder (part-owner) of the company and has no rights. He receives no dividends and loses his *entire investment* if the stock does not make it to the exercise price.

For illustration: The Greyhound Corporation (symbol G.) has a warrant, The Greyhound Corp. '80, trading on the Big Board with the following conditions. The company guarantees to deliver *one* share of common stock for each warrant held at an Exercise Price (E.P.) of $23.50 at any time up to 5/14/80. At the time this is written, these warrants may be bought for 1.6 (1 5/8). The parent stock is trading at 11.6 (11 5/8). Why would anyone pay $1.6 for something that is basically worthless (since the common stock is below the exercise price and pays no dividends)? The stock has, it would seem, to reach 23.5 (exercise price) and 1.6 (price paid) = 25.1 for the warrant buyer to break even. However, let us compare what happens to the buyer of 100 shares of common stock vs. the same amount of money put into warrants. 100 shares G. at 11.6 = $1160 (we will ignore commissions). Imagine that G. has a nice move to 23.2. The profit, if the position is closed out, is:

$$\frac{23.2 - 11.6}{11.6} \quad x \quad 100 = 100\% \quad = \text{ nice going.}$$

Notice that at 23.2 the warrants are still below the exercise price of 23.5. However, because of the length of time remaining it is certain that such warrants would be trading around 5 or 6. Let's pick 5.6 (their actual price would be subject to all the factors that affect the market). Now the same $1160 that bought 100 shares of *G.* at 11.6, would buy *725 warrants at 1.6.* The profit in this situation would be:

$$\frac{(5.6 - 1.6)\ 7.25}{11.6} \quad x \quad 100 = 250\%.$$

This is *leverage.* This explains why people buy warrants. Note that the warrant which is traded at 5.6 is still basically worthless as the common stock, *on which the warrant depends,* is still below the exercise price of 23.5. Such a warrant has no *intrinsic value* therefore; it is all premium. If G. rose to 30, the warrant price would trade around 10. Under these conditions 30 – 23.5 (exercise price) = 6.5 would be *intrinsic value* and 10.0 – 6.5 = 3.5 would be *premium.*

It is important to grasp this concept as *options,* which play an important part in my Moving Balance System, are also, basically, *very short-term warrants.* There are some differences which will become apparent, but an option that is in-the-money (to use the vernacular) is one that has *intrinsic value* plus premium. One that is out-of-the-money is *all premium.* The amount of premium investors are prepared to pay will vary with all the conditions that affect the market generally, and is usually higher in a bull market.

To return to the original example, let's imagine that at expiration date, G. common stock is at 44.50. Since warrants are a *wasting asset*, to the extent that on expiration date all premium will have disappeared, how would the situation—stock purchase vs. same amount of money put into purchase of warrants—have made out?

1) **Stock Purchase**

	Debit	Credit
100 shares G. at 11.6	1160.	
sold at 44.5		4450.

$$\text{Profit} = \frac{\$4450. - \$1160.}{\$1160} \times 100 = 284\%$$

2) **Warrant Purchase**

725 warrants at 1.6	1160.	
With the stock at 44.50 the warrant is worth 44.50 – 23.50 (E.P.) = 21.00		
received therefore is 725 x 21.00 =		15,225.

$$\text{Profit} = \frac{\$15,225 - \$1160.}{\$1160.} \times 100 = 1213\%$$

The other side of the story should be mentioned. By 1980 it is unlikely that the Greyhound Corporation will have gone broke and so the 100 shares would in all probability have some value whereas the warrants would expire *entirely worthless* if the stock closed at any point below 23.5 on expiration date. The warrant purchaser would lose the entire amount of his speculation.

Thorp and Kassouf came up with a system—they called it their basic system—which was designed to give a good deal of protection as well as profit. It is based on the following idea. All warrants have, as we have seen, a premium that diminishes as the expiration date approaches—to disappear altogether on that date. *This premium can be sold short as it is bound to disappear.* Selling short is fully explained in Chapter 11, but, briefly, it involves *selling* a security you have *borrowed* and buying it later in the open market to return to the lender. Obviously, if you can buy it for less than you sold it for (if, that is, the security has *fallen* in value) you make a profit which is the difference between what you received and what you had to pay. If the stock, however, *rises*, you will (at some time) have to buy it in the market to return it to its owner and you will *lose* money.

Let us consider for a moment the situation in which I had my other success. Texas International Petroleum (symbol TIP) had a warrant out as follows: Exercise Price 9, Expiration Date 5/31/74. One warrant to be a call on (be exchanged for) one share of common stock at the exercise price. At the time I took my original position the common stock sold for 8.4 and the warrant for 4.6. It seems at first crazy for anyone to pay 4.6 for a warrant without intrinsic value when they could buy the parent stock for 8.4. But, above the sum of the Exercise Price, plus what was paid for the warrant (9.0 + 4.6 = 13.6), the warrant will increase point for point with the common stock. Leverage again. However, since the warrant is all premium which will diminish throughout its life to disappear entirely on expiration date, why not sell it short as follows?

		Debit	Credit
(1) Buy	100 shares TIP	840	
(2) Sell (short)	100 TIP warrants		460*

(* consult Chapter 11 for the margin requirements
and the way this is carried on the books).

This situation is a *true* hedge as the long position and the short position are held in securities, one of which is convertible into the other.

What would happen if at expiration date the stock was exactly at the Exercise Price? Clearly the warrants, each of which represents the right to buy one share of common stock at 9, would be worthless. So a profit will be made on both sides.

At *9* therefore, the Buy Side will show the following profit:

BUY SIDE

Debit	Credit
840	900

Profit = <u>0.6 points</u>

and the Sell Side will also show a profit (as the warrants will be worthless):

SELL SIDE

	Debit	Credit
Warrants are worthless	0	460

Profit = 4.6 points
Total Profit = 4.6 + 0.6 = <u>5.2 points</u>

Note that on the Sell Side the warrants can be "covered" at negligible cost and the *4.6 points received is profit*. In fact, when the mix is 1:1 (No. warrants sold short vs. 100 shares stock held long) the maximum profit will be at the exercise or *any point above the exercise price*.

Let's consider the situation that would occur if the stock closed at 40 on the expiration date.

At *40* therefore, the Buy Side will show the following profit:

BUY SIDE

Debit	Credit
840	4000

Profit = 40 – 8.4
         = <u>31.6 points</u>

and the Sell Side the following loss (as each warrant will be worth 40 – 9 = 31):

SELL SIDE

Debit	Credit
3100	460

Loss = 31 – 4.6
        = 26.4 points
Overall Profit = 31.6 – 26.4
                 = <u>5.2 points</u>

Figure 2 depicts the situation and shows the downside risk. The downside breakeven point = X (commissions have been ignored though they play a very real part in the actual mathematics). X will equal the stock price paid (SPP) less the warrant price received (WPR) = 8.4 – 4.6 = 3.8.

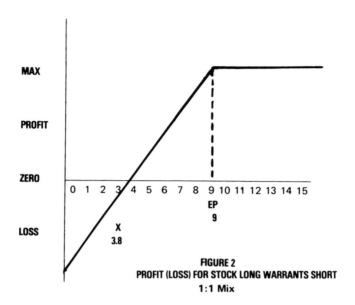

FIGURE 2
PROFIT (LOSS) FOR STOCK LONG WARRANTS SHORT
1:1 Mix

At *3.8* therefore, the Sell Side will show the following profit (as the warrants will be worthless):

SELL SIDE

Debit	Credit
0	460

Profit = <u>4.6 points</u>

and the Buy Side the following loss:

BUY SIDE

Debit	Credit
840	380

Loss = <u>4.6 points</u>

The Formula is:

Formula 1 To find downside breakeven point "X" in a mix where stock is held long, and warrants are held short.

Downside breakeven point = X

Stock Price Paid = SPP

Warrant Price Received = WPR

Mix = No. warrants sold short ÷ No. shares stock purchased

X = SPP – (WPR) mix

So this position would yield in this mix a profit if at expiration the stock was anywhere from 3.8 to infinity.

By varying the Mix one can profit even if the stock declines to zero. For example,

		Debit	Credit
(1)	Buy <u>100</u> shares TIP at 8.4	840	
(2)	Sell short <u>200</u> warrants at 4.6		920
			(4.6 x 2)

The mix is now <u>2 to 1</u>.

If TIP falls to zero you still make 9.2 – 8.4 = 0.8 points. The downside breakeven point (X) in this case is at minus 0.8. Fortunately, though stocks may fall to zero value, that's as low as they can go. But the price one pays for *increased downside protection* in a hedge is *decreased upside protection*. In this case, a 2:1 mix, the upside breakeven point which we will call "B", is given by the following formula:

Formula 2 To find upside breakeven point "B" in mix stock long, warrants short.

Upside breakeven point = B

Stock Price Paid = SPP

Mix = No. warrants sold short ÷ No. shares stock purchased

Exercise Price = EP

Warrant Price Received = WPR

B – SPP = (B – (EP + WPR)) mix

i.e. $B - 8.4 = (B - (9 + 4.6)) \, 2$

$B - 8.4 = 2 \, B - (13.6) \, 2$

$= 2 \, B - 27.2$

Add 27.2 to each side: $27.2 + B - 8.4 = 2 \, B$

Subtract B from each side: $27.2 - 8.4 = B$

$B = 27.2 - 8.4 = \mathit{18.8}$

At 18.8 therefore, the Buy Side will show the following profit:

BUY SIDE

	Debit	Credit
Profit = 18.8 – 8.4 = <u>10.4 points</u>	840	1880

and the Sell Side the following loss (as each warrant is now worth 9.8):

SELL SIDE

	Debit	Credit
Note warrant is worth	1960	920
18.8 – EP		
18.8 – 9 = 9.8	(9.8 x 2)	(4.6 x 2)
Loss = 19.6 – 9.2 = <u>10.4 points</u>		

This can be shown graphically in Figure 3.

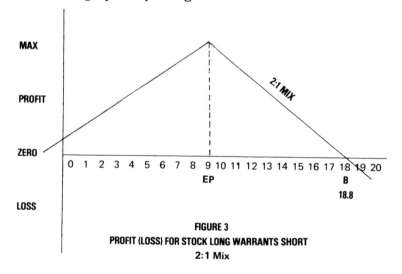

FIGURE 3
PROFIT (LOSS) FOR STOCK LONG WARRANTS SHORT
2:1 Mix

There are several points I would like to make.

1) The maximum profit is *always* exactly at the Exercise Price.

2) If the warrant is exchangeable on a ratio other than 1 share common stock for each warrant tended, both the exercise price and the warrant price will have to be *adjusted* accordingly. Since I do not recommend warrant hedging, I am not going to go into this further. Anyone interested should consult Thorp and Kassouf, or Nodding's book, *The Dow Jones—Irwin Guide To Convertible Securities.*

3) I personally have derived all the formulae I have given in this book—not because I wanted to particularly, but because I needed them and could not find them anywhere.

4) Thorp and Kassouf call the situation long stock, short warrants, a warrant hedge and the other way around—long warrants, short stock, a reversed warrant hedge. This is the way these terms are used in this book. It is unfortunate that some other writers use the term reverse warrant hedge for the hedge stock long, warrants short, *so be warned.*

In a 2:1 mix therefore, some profit will be made if, at expiration date, the common is anywhere between 0 and 18.8. The maximum profit will always be exactly at the Exercise Price. This characteristic will be seen again when we consider certain types of option hedge.

I do not recommend warrant hedging for a number of reasons:

a) Recently corporations have taken to extending the life of outstanding warrants (in order to avoid paying taxes, the I.R.S. recently having changed its ruling on warrants). This acts to the detriment of the short seller of warrants.

b) The waiting period is long. If real money is to be made in the market it must be made by riding the swings. A hedged position protects against loss but does not develop a substantial profit rapidly.

c) The possibility of a short squeeze (see Chap. 11), or being bought in does exist.

d) There often is difficulty in finding warrants to borrow in order to sell them short.

e) The margin requirements (see Chap. 11) for low priced warrants are unfavorable.

Nor do I recommend reversed warrant hedging (warrants long, stock short). This is basically a procedure for bull markets where appreciation is looked for in the larger number of warrants held long than the loss in the short position. It has the great disadvantage that the short seller is *charged* (debited) any dividends normally paid on the stock he holds short. This came as a big shock to me the first time it happened, as Thorp and Kassouf failed to give this information in the warrant section (though they mentioned it in the section on convertible bonds as I discovered later). But they did point out one interesting aspect of a reversed warrant hedge. If you wish to dazzle or confuse your broker quote section 220.3 (d) (3) of the Federal Reserve System Regulation T at him. This reads as follows:

> (3) The current market value of any securities (other than unissued securities) sold short in the general account plus, for each security (other than an exempted security), such amount as the Board shall prescribe from time to time in 220.8 (d) (the Supplement to Regulation T) as the margin required for such short sales, except that such amount so prescribed in such 220.8 (d) need not be included when there are held in the general account or special convertible debt security account the same securities or securities exchangeable or convertible within 90 calendar days, *without restriction other than the payment of money*, into such securities sold short;

It means, in effect, that margin is only required on the warrants bought long and that no margin is required against the short sale. It not only confuses your broker; it confuses the hell out of the margin clerk also as neither your broker nor the margin clerk are likely to be very familiar with the regulation. So it's good for one-upmanship if you are feeling a little diminished, but the reversed warrant hedge is better avoided unless you **really are** prepared to study it in the manner described by Noddings. Incidentally, knowledge of the above Regulation 220.3 (d) (3) can be very valuable in shorting stock to trade against convertible bonds and/or convertible preferreds, as the short side is in effect "free" (except for the commissions involved).

CHAPTER 5

JAZZING UP THE A/D INDEX

Jazzing Up The A/D Index

In the last chapter, the B/S and A/D Indices were derived and I remarked on the way they moved in unison. I have the figures to prove it and I hope you will accept my statement. Since the A/D Index is a good deal easier to calculate on a day to day basis, and also does not take up as much space (the B/S Index is derived from 4 sets of figures, the A/D from 2), I decided to concentrate on the A/D Index. What bothered me about this index (and this also applies to the B/S Index) was that the *volume of shares* traded was ignored. Volume fuels the market so I had to find some way of tracking it.

I noticed that Larry Williams had mentioned two indicators in his book, one dealing entirely in volume, the other in the number of issues traded as well as volume. These two indices were (1) the 10 day M.A. of the advancing volume; (2) the 10 day M.A. of the Trader's Index.

1) *The 10 day M.A. of the Advancing Volume*

This is derived, like any other 10 day Moving Average, from the number of shares advancing *on a 10 day basis.* The average is of the actual *number of shares* that moved up, *not* the number of advancing *issues.* The figures are given in any good daily newspaper under the heading "Volume Statistics." It tends to get tucked into any old odd corner on the financial pages and sometimes is not to be found at all (call your broker). Barron's lists it weekly (though not in a regular place in the paper and not always) in a box headed:

Stock Exchange Volume Trends
(shares, 000 omitted).

For instance,

Stock Exchange Volume Trends
(shares, 000 omitted)

			NYSE			AMEX		NASDAQ	
		Up	Down	QCHA (%)	Up	Down	QCHA (%)	Up	Down
October	28	4,290	4,530	– .36	800	500	–.37	1,079	1,756
	29	11,820	2,360	+1.41	1,100	500	+.63	3,457	775
	30	14,080	4,090	+1.01	1,350	890	+.48	3,359	1,047
	31	7,980	7,870	– .10	760	940	+.31	3,110	1,183
Nov.	1	5,710	5,840	– .08	900	480	+.22	1,728	1,481

Supplied by QUOTRON.

In my daily newspaper, the volume statistics for November 1, 1974 (published on November 2nd) were listed as follows:

	Advanced	Declined
NYSE	5,736,600 shares	5,872,820
AMEX	902,820 shares	484,570

As with the A/D Index, we are only concerned with the New York Stock Exchange. Notice that the two sets of figures for the N.Y.S.E. do not correspond (daily newspaper vs. Barron's). This is of no consequence as we really do not need any great degree of accuracy. The moving average is kept with the thousands (-000) omitted (as in the Barron's statistics) and the final figure is always a zero. Since I use my daily paper for computing the figure, the figure I used for November 1st was *5740*. If I had used the Barron's figure, I would have used *5710*. I bring this out as it is sometimes a source of confusion—but it need not be, as what we are looking for are trends and the difference between 5740 and 5710 is of no importance. Just remember that the figure is corrected to 3 figures but 4 are used, the final one being zero. To give you an idea of the way the 10 day M.A. of the advancing volume runs, on November 1st the figure was 7146. This means that over the past 10 days the moving total of all the shares that advanced was 71,460,000. Drop three 0's = 71,460. Therefore, the 10 day M.A. is 7146. This figure fluctuates, in the two and a half years for which I have data, from a very low of 2523 (August 23, 1974) to a very high of 16200 (February 6, 1975). At the risk of being repetitious, I would like to make sure that I have gotten across that this M.A. deals *only* with the *total number of shares advancing.*

2) 	*The 10 day M.A. of the Trader's Index*

I have always listed this index in my notebooks as MKDS, which are the letters you can punch on the Bunker-Ramo Quote Machine to get the figure already calculated for you. The figure is derived as follows:

$$\frac{\text{No. of advancing issues}}{\text{No. of declining issues}} \div \frac{\text{advancing volume}}{\text{declining volume}}$$

or

$$\frac{\text{No. of advancing issues}}{\text{No. of declining issues}} \times \frac{\text{declining volume}}{\text{advancing volume}}$$

This index basically seeks an answer to the question, are the issues that are advancing getting their share of the volume? If they are, and because of the way the index is set up, then bullish readings will be *low* (below 0.9) and bearish readings will be high (over 1.1). Between 0.9 and 1.1 the territory is neutral. Let us consider the actual example of November 1, 1974.

NYSE

No. of issues advancing = 702
No. of issues declining = 664

This ratio is $\frac{702}{664} = 1.06.$

Now if there was as much interest in the advancing issues as the declining issues on a volume basis, the advancing volume ÷ declining volume would also be under these conditions of equal interest, 1.06 and the Trader's Index (MKDS) would be *1.0*. But what were the actual figures for the advancing and declining volume again?

$$\frac{\text{advancing volume}}{\text{declining volume}} = \frac{5,736,600}{5,872,820}$$

omitted three 0's and corrections to three figures:

$$= \frac{5740}{5870}$$

$$= 0.97.$$

This means that the issues that advanced did *not* get their full share of the volume and this is shown in the final figure 1.06/0.97 = 1.09. Actually, as I have said, this is really a neutral reading. The readings run on a daily basis from very bullish readings around 0.4, to very bearish readings around 2.30 (one highly unusual reading of 4.17 was given on 11/8/74).

A 10 day M.A. of the readings can be run in the usual way. It ranges from a high of 0.708 (April 21,1975), to an enormously bearish reading of 1.854 on October 3, 1974. Previous to this 10 day M.A. low, 1.463 was the lowest (on August 21, 1974). Though the figures cannot mean much to you at this point, a move of 0.391 (1.854 – 1.463) is a long move by any standards and, as a move *below a previous lowest*, had me ready for the rally that began on Monday, October 7th. In that one week the Dow rose a record 73.61 points. All I can say is that with an MKDS of 1.854 (an unheard of low in two year's action) what else was there to expect?

We now have three indicators:

1) The A/D Index
2) The 10 day M.A. of the Advancing Volume
3) The 10 day M.A. of the Trader's Index

These three indicators are derived from four sets of figures:

a) The number of issues that advanced
b) The number of issues that declined
c) The advancing volume
d) The declining volume

Indicator (1) uses (a) and (b)
Indicator (2) uses (c) only
Indicator (3) uses (a) (b) (c) and (d).

My idea was to try and refine the A/D Index, so that a single composite index was produced. Obviously, what was wanted was an indicator that could tell me *right now* where I was. After all, any goon can look *back* over the past action of the stock market and pick out highs and lows *once they have been made,* with exquisite precision. What I wanted to know was, (and is) where am I?

(5) up, absolutely primed to go down
(4) up, intermediate high?
(3) sideways
(2) down, intermediate low?
(1) down, absolutely primed to go up

These correspond, as we shall see, to five zones which I will describe later. Zone 5 being up, absolutely primed to go down—i.e. heavily overbought; and Zone 1 being down, absolutely primed to go up—i.e. heavily oversold.

It was somewhere about the middle of 1973 that I realized something that should have been obvious long before, and now seems so obvious that I almost hesitate to write about it. There are really only two trends in the market one has to worry about, no matter what the time cycle experts say. One is the short term movement that happens to be clearly shown by the 10 day moving averages (maybe because it encompasses two weeks of market activity or maybe because the mathematics are easy), and the other is everything longer than this movement. The intermediate and long term trends can be up, down or sideways, but like electrons around a nucleus, the 10 day moving averages gyrate around them and, all things considered, they do so with remarkable regularity.

Remember that everything that happens has to do so originally on a daily basis.

Clearly, if the long term trend is up, the distance from a short term *low* to a short term *high* will be greater than that from a short term *high* to a short term *low* and similarly when the long term trend is down, the reverse will hold true (Figure 4). One of the surprising things I learned is that the market will always find an excuse for behaving more or less in balance with the 10 day moving averages. Sometimes, the excuses are logical; Watergate, impeachment, prime rate increases, drought, etc. But at other times, they are totally illogical and as such, are described as technical corrections, investor optimism, or in terms of a response to a completely insignificant piece of news.

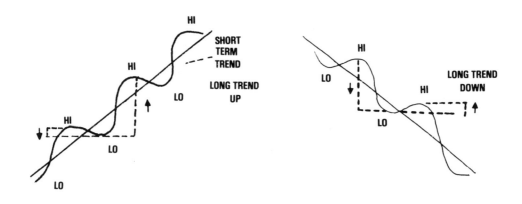

FIGURE 4
HOW THE MARKET MOVES UP AND DOWN

Sometimes, however, the state of the market becomes unbalanced. When this occurs, the indices move *decisively* into overbought (or oversold) territory and *may stay there for some time.* Caution: the higher (and to a lesser extent lower) they go, the longer they may stay unbalanced. But as night follows day (and day, night) a reversal occurs and balance is restored.

When studying the B/S Index, I picked arbitrarily 70% buyers, 30% sellers (B/S Index 2.33) as overbought and 30% buyers, 70% sellers (B/S Index 0.43) as oversold. We saw how these held up in practice. Most of market activity occurs, I have found, between the normal limits of 65% buyers, 35% sellers and 35% buyers and 65% sellers. What I wanted to find, if I could, was a way of spotting when the market would move significantly into overbought and oversold territory. It is important to realize that this *cannot be done.* I have found that in a normal trading market, one without marked emotional reactions, the points of reversal can be picked with far greater precision than they can in the kind of super-charged market like the one that began in December 1974 and gained at a record annualized rate of around 170%. There is no way to spot a trend such as this *at its inception* or even after it has moved into normally overbought territory. What happens is that, for reasons known (regular prime rate cuts, lots of institutional money to invest) and reasons unknown, the market becomes markedly unbalanced, and, like an elephant on tip-toe, it manages to hold the pose for longer than seems feasible. So when a really significant degree of imbalance occurs, all one can hope to identify is a reversal *area* and one can miss the actual reversal point by as much as 50-60 points on the Dow.

As you see, I wanted to try and pick exact reversal points, but the market won't let itself be pinned down that accurately. However, if you wait until climactic readings are reached you can plunk your money down and bet on a reversal occuring in due course. Consider the following facts:

1) The A/D Index most of the time reverses with readings around 1.55 on the high side and 0.65 on the down side. It moves back and forth between these two levels, but from time to time something happens to upset the balance and unusually high (or low) readings are recorded (2.46 versus 0.42). I call these unusual readings big wave reversal points as by this time it was obvious to me that the market movement was one of flow.

2) The 10 day M.A. of the advancing volume also varies from a regular high of around 8000 to a regular low around 4000 in bear markets and 11,000 and 6000 in bull markets. It also took off occasionally into high volume territory—16200 was my all time high and into low volume territory, 2523 my all time low.

3) The 10 day M.A. of MKDS also fluctuated between 0.950 high and 1.350 low

in similar small wave fashion with big wave readings as high as 0.708 and big wave lows as low as 1.854 (I still can't get over that reading). Well, if I could imagine the market fluctuating gently between the usual reversal points (Figure 5), could I devise some sort of handle on its balance and, therefore, identify big wave reversal areas if not the actual points (Figure 6)? Perhaps I could put these three indicators together in some meaningful way and call the one indicator I had devised the *moving balance indicator* (M.B.I.); because if I could get that, then surely I should be able to develop a *moving balance system*.

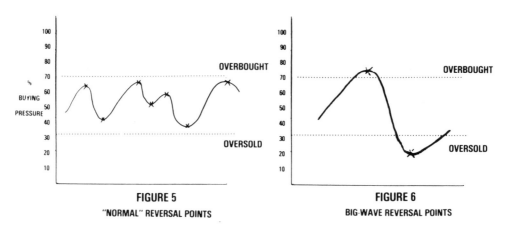

Well it became obvious that, to use the zone concept again, if the market was, say, in Zone 4, an *intermediate high* with the possibility of going higher but with the greater possibility of going lower, all one needed was faith and patience because the pattern of behavior was either Zone 4 to *3* to 2 to 3 to 4—or Zone 4 to *5* to 4 to 1 (often) to 2 to 3 to 4. I have the figures to prove it. Therefore, as part of the moving balance concept it seemed to me that all I had to do was make sure (1) that I only *initiated* transactions when the Market was in Zone 4 or 5 for *short* positions and in Zone 2 or 1 for *long* positions and (2) that I had some kind of protective mechanism in case the market went against me. Actually, an opening position taken at 4 and held while the stock went into Zone 5 and then back through 4 and lower would have had a profitable outcome a clear majority of the time. But it is uncomfortable—particularly for someone of high volatility index—to have a stock go against one. Therefore, *I had to find a hedge*. But, before that, I had to devise a way of getting these three indicators together to give me one significant indicator to guide me. I felt it should be possible to get one as the three indicators were derived, as I have shown, from four determinants. Here's how I found my *moving balance indicator.*

CHAPTER 6

THE MOVING BALANCE INDICATOR— PASSPORT TO TRANQUILITY

Chapter 6

The Moving Balance Indicator—
Passport To Tranquility

As I described in the last chapter, three 10 day indicators (A/D Index, 10 day M.A. advancing volume, and 10 day M.A. MKDS) have to be kept on a daily basis. Let us go back to the beginning of 1974 and study the *A/D Index* for the first 10 trading days of 1974.

TABLE I: A/D INDEX

			Adv.	Decl.	10 day M.A. Adv.	10 day M.A. Decl.	A/D Index	
Jan.	2	1	1070	431	871.2	650.5	1.34	
1974	3	2	1565	152	930.5	613.1	1.52	
	4	3	1039	527	959.6	591.6	1.61	
	7	4	899	640	981.6	574.4	1.71	▼
	8	5	487	1053	971.6	587.7	1.65	
	9	6	246	1314	929.4	645.2	1.44	
	10	7	478	977	856.7	707.1	1.21	
	11	8	986	469	837.2	709.1	1.18	
	14	9	797	648	849.5	686.9	1.23	
	15	10	822	583	838.8	679.4	1.24	

The A/D Index, as we saw in the last chapter, is devised as follows:

10 day M.A. advances ÷ 10 day M.A. declines

69

As such, though it is based on two 10 day M.A., it is not itself a moving average. It is a figure that has to be calculated directly each day. But obviously, being based on two moving averages, it gives information on a moving average basis. Please notice also that you will not be able to devise the two 10 day M.A.'s yourself from the above table, as I do not give the relevant preceding figures. You may accept the figures as they are given, as they are accurate. The topping out process of the A/D Index can be clearly seen on January 7th. Actually, 1.71 was the high on the A/D Index in 1974 until a higher reading was made on October 14, 1974 (2.03). As such, 1.71, it is a big wave high, as we shall see. It can be flagged in one's notes as a solid triangle pointed down (▼).

During the same period, the *10 day M.A. of the Advancing Volume* gave readings as follows:

TABLE II: 10 DAY M. A. OF THE ADVANCING VOLUME

		Adv. Vol.	10 day M.A. Adv. Vol.
Jan.	2	6850	9618
1974	3	21790	10572
	4	9940	10741
	7	8530	10854 ▼
	8	3740	10403
	9	1280	10098
	10	4020	9063
	11	9500	8442
	14	6950	8437
	15	7510	8011

The 10 day M.A. of the advancing volume also topped out on Jan. 7, therefore, and is so flagged. Note that, for a top to be called, three lower readings on either side are necessary. The same holds in reverse for a bottom, 3 higher readings on either side. This is flagged by an empty triangle pointing upwards (△).

What was the *Trader's Index* (MKDS) doing during this period? Remember *low* readings of the MKDS Index are bullish, and *high* readings are bearish. The figures are as follows (and again you will not be able to actually calculate the moving averages, as I do not give the previous figures. But there is nothing difficult about a 10 day M.A., I assure you).

TABLE III: MKDS—10 DAY M. A. MKDS

		MKDS	10 day M.A. MKDS
Jan.	2	1.47	1.037
1974	3	1.00	1.069
	4	1.83	1.135
	7	1.37	1.187
	8	1.61	1.224
	9	2.32	1.348
	10	1.29	1.416
	11	1.01	1.434 △
	14	1.12	1.400
	15	0.74	1.376

Now these figures are very interesting, as the 10 day M.A. of the MKDS made a *low* of 1.434 on January 11th when the other indicators made *highs* on January 7th. What is going on? After all, I have claimed readings around 1.4 as distinctly bearish and yet here we are at an intermediate high, at least, with one of the indicators, the MKDS, markedly bearish.

Let us go back to December 27, 1973. The 10 day M.A. of the MKDS topped out on December 27th with a reading of 0.978. The reason for the dissociation between the MKDS and the two other indicators is that when the market gets unbalanced, heavy volume comes in and this may weight the MKDS equation toward the bearish side. Indeed, *dislocation between the MKDS and the other readings is a valuable indicator of imbalance in the market.*

Interestingly enough, the 10 day M.A. of the MKDS didn't get into the 1.434 territory again until August 21, 1974. However, on that occasion the volume pattern was quite different, there being very low volume (10 day M.A. of advancing vol. 2745). The conclusions to be drawn are, therefore, that bearish readings of the 10 day M.A. MKDS: (1) indicate market imbalance (when volume is high and the other indicators are bullish) and a possible reversal, (2) actually indicate an intermediate *low* when volume is low.

Well, if I was going to put these three indicators together, could I somehow get these facts about the MKDS into the equation? I tried all sorts of ways, but finally decided just to note in my own mind any discordancy between the MKDS and the other indicators as *an indication of imbalance* and to include the MKDS figures, in some way, into the equation without applying a correction. Again, I tried several ways of doing this as the other indicators are direct indicators (up = up) whereas the MKDS is a reciprocal indicator (down = up). Finally, I hit on the following table. The 10 day M.A. of the MKDS figures run from a very bullish 0.798 = 0.8 to a very bearish 1.854 = 1.85. I decided to treat them as shown in the following table; and assign to each 10 day M.A. reading a value, rounding off both sets of figures.

TABLE IV: 10 DAY M. A. MKDS—ASSIGNED VALUE

10 day M.A. MKDS	ASSIGNED VALUE
(to nearest 0.05)	
0.75	8.5
0.80	8.0
0.85	7.5
0.90	7.0
0.95	6.5
1.00	6 0
1.05	5.5
1.10	5.0
1.15	4.5
1.20	4.0
1.25	3.5
1.30	3.0
1.35	2.5
1.40	2.0
1.45	1.5
1.50	1.0
1.55	0.5
1.60	0
1.65	− 0.5
1.70	− 1.0
1.75	− 1.5
1.80	− 2.0
1.85	− 2.5

Now I had all three indicators related positively to market action and the moving balance indicator (M.B.I.) could be devised. This is done as follows:

Step I   take the A/D Index reading and multiply by 10, i.e., on Jan. 2 the A/D Index was 1.34, multiply by 10 = *13.4*.

Step II   take the 10 day M.A. of the advancing volume figures, divide by 1000 and correct to one place of decimals. The 10 day M.A. figure on January 2 was 9618.

i.e. $9618 \div 1000 = 9.618$
$$= 9.6$$

Now,

Step III find the assigned figures for the 10 day M.A. of the MKDS for January 2.

$$10 \text{ day M.A. MKDS} = 1.037 = 1.05$$
$$= 5.5$$

Step IV add all these figures together

$$13.4$$
$$9.6$$
$$5.5$$
$$\overline{28.5}$$

Step V multiply this figure by 2 and correct to the nearest whole number:
$$28.5 \text{ x } 2 = 57$$

The moving balance indicator readings for the 10 trading days, January 2 thru January 15, therefore are as follows:

TABLE V: MOVING BALANCE INDICATOR READINGS

		A/D	10 day Adv. Vol.	10 day MKDS	Total	T x 2 M.B.I.
Jan.	2	13.4	9.6	5.5	28.5	57
	3	15.2	10.6	5.5	31.3	63
	4	16.1	10.7	4.5	31.3	63
	7	17.1	10.9	4.0	32.0	64
	8	16.5	10.4	4.0	31.8	62
	9	14.4	10.1	2.5	27.0	54
	10	12.1	9.1	2.0	23.2	46
	11	11.8	8.4	1.5	21.7	43
	14	12.3	8.4	2.0	22.7	45
	15	12.4	8.0	2.0	22.4	45

The M.B.I. figures therefore provide an overview of the market. The reasons for multiplying by 2 are: (1) to round off the numbers to the nearest whole number more easily and accurately, (2) to bring the values into line with the % buying pressure I have already discussed. You will remember the highest reading on the B/S Index was 2.1. This is equivalent to 68% buyers ÷ 32% sellers = 2.1. Notice that the figure of 68% "buyers" (or if you prefer "buying pressure") relates nicely to the M.B.I. high of 64 just devised for January 7th.

For those who may wonder "why not just use the B/S Index, why bother with Lloyd's M.B.I.," my answer is succinctly "increased sensitivity." There are occasions when following the B/S Index, or the A/D Index, alone, fails to reveal the whole story, and when following the M.B.I. gives a better representation of what's going on. We shall see some examples of this later.

Whereas the three indicators (1) A/D, (2) 10 day M.A. advancing volume, and (3) 10 day M.A. MKDS *have* to be followed and computed daily, it is sufficient to compute the M.B.I. three times a week: Monday, Wednesday, Friday. Only if a high is made on Tuesday or Thursday need the figure be computed on either of these days. In a 4 day trading week, Wednesday and Friday readings of the M.B.I. suffice. The figures are computed only 3 times a week, as they stand out better this way without losing any sensitivity. Of course, when market action is planned it is essential to work out the latest figure.

TABLE VI
M. B. I. REVERSAL POINTS

		HIGH				LOW	
	Date	M.B.I.	N.Y. Comp.		Date	M.B.I.	N.Y. Comp.
1973	1/ 9/73	66	65.3		2/ 2/73	32	61.8
	2/13/73	44	62.9		2/28/73	28	60.0
	3/13/73	48	61.3		3/22/73	27	58.1
	4/19/73	50	59.6		4/27/73	29	56.9
	5/ 9/73	47	58.6		5/21/73	25	54.2
	5/30/73	43	55.4		6/25/73	26	53.8
	7/23/73	67	57.3		8/21/73	24	53.8
	9/27/73	80	58.8		12/ 3/73	28	50.0
1974	1/ 7/74	64	52.5		1/21/74	37	51.0
	1/24/74	56	51.7		2/13/74	28	48.7
	3/ 5/74	64	52.2		4/ 9/74	21	49.3
	4/17/74	38	50.2		4/30/74	28	47.9
	5/ 9/74	44	49.1		5/24/74	24	45.9
	6/ 7/74	54	48.7		7/10/74	17	41.7
	7/24/74	55	44.5		8/ 2/74	30	41.2
	8/ 9/74	38	42.4		8/23/74	17	37.6
	9/ 6/74	32	37.3		9/16/74	23	34.6
	9/25/74	38	35.6		10/ 4/74	16	32.9
	10/18/74	69	38.1		10/28/74	35	37.0
	11/11/74	61	39.8		11/21/74	22	36.2
1975	1/13/75	76	38.4		1/21/75	49	37.7
	2/ 5/75	85	42.0		2/28/75	52	43.1
	3/11/75	76	44.6		4/ 7/75	36	42.7
	4/21/75	78	46.2		5/ 1/75	51	46.6
	5/14/75	72	48.8		5/29/75	46	47.7

Table VI gives the M.B.I. reversal points (*all* the points, not just the big wave reversal points) in 1973, 1974, and the first half of 1975. The New York Stock Exchange Composite Index (N.Y. Comp.) is plotted for comparison (corrected to the first place of decimals). It is important to realize that the N.Y. Comp. figures relate to M.B.I. reversal points, and not to reversal points on the New York

Composite Index itself.

One of the first facts to observe is that the Moving Balance Indicator moves in harmony with the market. Remember, the M.B.I. is trying to forecast the next few weeks of market activity. In bear years (1973, 1974) notice that all short positions taken at M.B.I. highs would have been profitable if the New York Comp. were to be treated as a single stock, and that all, save one, of the low points (8/23/74) were followed by a higher New York Comp. value at the next M.B.I. high.

The dramatic change in market direction in 1975 can be clearly seen from the readings. There are two significant facts:

1) Both high and low reversal points on the M.B.I. have significantly higher values in 1975 than in the other years.

2) A strong bull signal was given on 2/28/75, when the M.B.I. reversed at a New York Comp. value *higher* (43.1) than the value at the previous M.B.I. high (42.0). This combination of a very high M.B.I. reading (85), followed by a reversal at higher N.Y. Comp. value, left me in no doubt about the strong upward momentum of the market. "We are going higher" I wrote in my notebook, and we certainly did.

It is instructive to compare the market action associated with the two very high M.B.I. readings of 80 (9/27/73) and 85 (2/5/75).

On 9/27/73, the N.Y. Comp. value was 58.8 when the M.B.I. was 80. The closing high of the N.Y. Comp. was 60.3 made on 10/12/73 when the M.B.I. was 65. The M.B.I. then fell all the way to 28. A short position taken at the M.B.I. high would have been very profitable. This particular rally has been termed a bear-market rally.

On 2/5/75, the N.Y. Comp. value was 42.0 when the M.B.I. was 85. The closing high of the N.Y. Comp. was 43.7 when the M.B.I. was 63. In both cases, the M.B.I. topped out 11 or 12 trading days before the market. (We will examine this phenomenon in detail in Chapter 10). However, in 1975, as we have just seen, the M.B.I. reversed at a higher reading on the N.Y. Comp. than at the previous **M.B.I.** high. This did *not* happen in 1973 when the M.B.I. just kept on falling. The assumption was, therefore, that the 1975 rally was *not* a bear market rally but a true new bull market.

Table VII gives the M.B.I. readings for the entire year 1974 calculated for Monday, Wednesday and Friday. When a reversal was made on either a Tuesday or a Thursday, this figure is given also.

TABLE VII
M.B.I. readings for 1974

Week Beginning	Mon.	Tues.	Wed.	Thurs.	Fri.
December 31, 1973	(53)		57		63
January 7, 1974	64 ▼		54		43
January 14	45		47		38
January 21	37 △		52	56 ▼	53
January 28	52		50		46
February 4	40		35		33
February 11	29		28 △		34
February 19	—		43		48
February 25	52		62		59
March 4	56	64 ▼	63		57
March 11	59		57		59
March 18	52		43		41
March 25	37		32		24
April 1	26		28		24
April 8	—		21 △		28
April 15	30		38 ▼		36
April 22	38		31		32
April 29	32	28 △	29		29
May 6	30		40	44 ▼	40
May 13	39		34		31
May 20	30		26	24 △	30
May 28	—		27		30
June 3	36		42		54 ▼
June 10	51		53		48
June 17	41		32		24
June 24	22		23		21
July 1	23		23		23
July 8	21		17 △		30
July 15	32		37		41
July 22	46		55 ▼		42
July 29	37		33		30
August 5	31		35		38
August 12	37		34		31
August 19	28		19		17 △
August 26	22		23		28

continued on following page.

TABLE VII *(continued)*

Week Beginning	Mon.	Tues.	Wed.	Thurs.	Fri.
September 3	—		22		32 ▼
September 9	31		29		25
September 16	23 △		34		34
September 23	37		38 ▼		37
September 30	31		27		16 △
October 7	22		33		54
October 14	67		58		69 ▼
October 21	65		51		40
October 28	35		49		46
November 4	41		53		58
November 11	61		45		42
November 18	33		24	22 △	24
November 25	22		30		30
December 2	25		36		30
December 9	28		31		29
December 16	32		38		43
December 23	39				39
December 30	39	47			

The M.B.I. figures actually pack more punch when they are charted. Figure 7 gives the figures for 1974. To return to the zone concept:

Bear Market Zones

Zone 5 *Up, absolutely primed to go down* can be drawn from 60 up.

Zone 4 *Up, intermediate high* runs from 60 to around 49.

Zone 3 *Sideways* from 49 down to 30

Zone 2 *Down, intermediate low*—runs from 30 to 21.

Zone 1 *Down, absolutely primed to go up* can be drawn below 21.

All well and good, but clearly Figure 7 does not show what the market was doing and though it looks pretty, is it of any use?

As far as its relevance to the market is concerned, I have inserted the actual M.B.I. reversal figures on a daily simplified chart of the Dow for 1974 (Figure 8). Certain very interesting things become apparent from study of these two charts; (1) when a rally occurs and the M.B.I. fails to make it to the previous high figure, a decline is imminent. A good example of this is the rally in the early part of August that carried the Dow almost to its previous high (July 23), and yet failed to score more than 38 while doing so (Previous high 55); (2) A high that scores

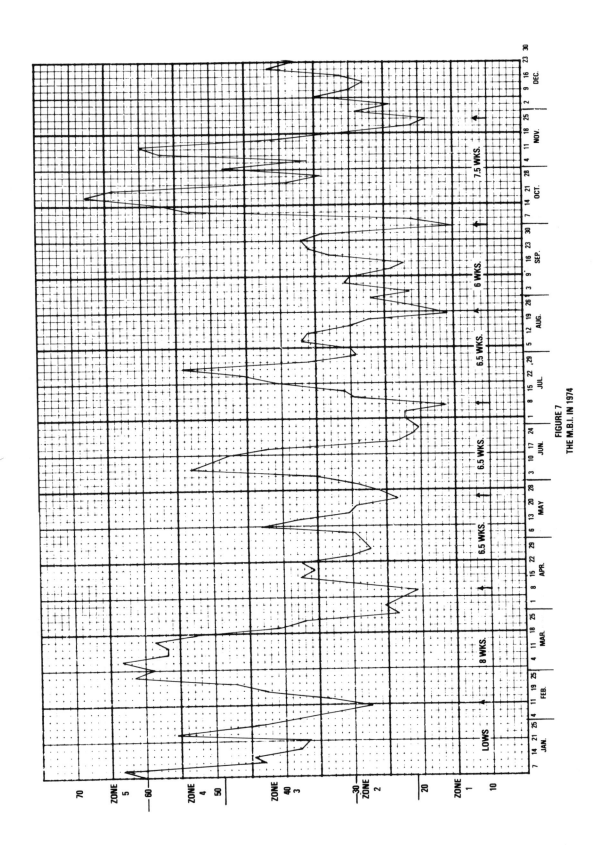

FIGURE 7
THE M.B.I. IN 1974

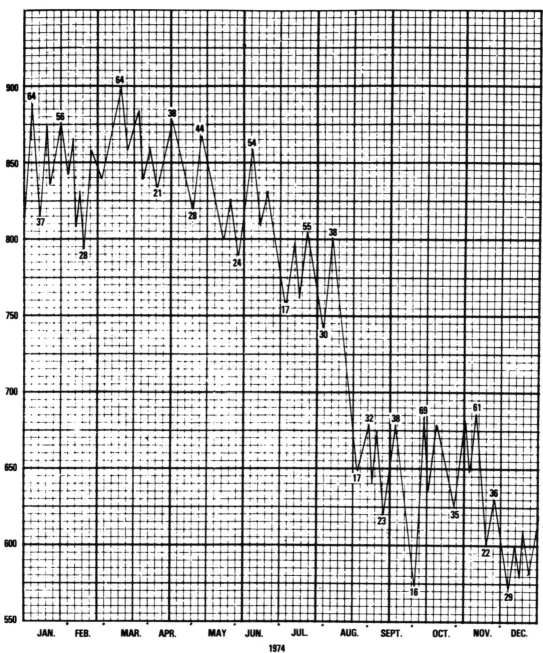

1974
FIGURE 8
M.B.I. READINGS RELATED TO DAILY
ACTION OF THE DOW IN 1974
(HIGH – LOW POINTS)

80

well on the M.B.I. (i.e., July 23 high of 55), and yet remains well below a previous high on the Dow with *similar M.B.I. readings* is a *bear* market rally and a strong indicator of worse to come. The figures in 1973 are similar, but I do not have any earlier figures. Obviously, the above statements are open to criticism on this ground, but I have confidence that the relationships between the M.B.I. and the Dow are real and meaningful and that the M.B.I. can therefore act not only as a short-term intermediate timing device but also give valuable longer term information as well; (3) The M.B.I., as we have seen, tends to turn down *before* the market does (because of the *high volume involved in buying sprees*), but calls the upturns from oversold territory very closely. "Be slow to turn bearish, quick to turn bullish." I have indicated market lows on Figure 7. Since I have only plotted 2 out of 5 trading days, the actual intervals are longer than they appear. The lows correspond to a 7 week periodicity. Gerald Appel, author of *Winning Market Systems* and editor of Systems and Forecasts, an advisory service, recently introduced a new trading oscillator, the 12 day trading oscillator calculated as follows. On Friday, October 11th, for example, the NYSE Index closed at 37.49. The indicator is worked out by subtracting from this the closing price of the NYSE Index 12 days previously counting Thursday, October 10th, as day 1 and going back 12 trading days to September 25th when the NYSE Index closed at 35.61. The oscillator reading is $37.49 - 35.61 = +1.88$. He showed that this oscillator also had a marked 7 week periodicity (Figure 9). Why not just use this simple 12 day oscillator and not the M.B.I.? The answer I think is that the M.B.I. can give a good idea of the longer term direction of the market, as we have seen, and also that once one gets used to keeping the three 10 day indicators, calculation of the M.B.I. is a matter of additional seconds only (with a calculator). At any rate, knowledge that such cycles occur is very useful and is incorporated into my Moving Balance System via the M.B.I.; (4) Climactic lows—big wave lows—will reverse, but that does not, unfortunately, mean that they will fuel a substantial rise if the overall market climate is unfavorable. The very oversold reading of 17 on August 23rd really did not move the market up much before it declined even further. One important point to observe was that a M.B.I. indicator of 17 was also made on July 10th when the market was 100 points higher. This one did call a significant reversal point but not a real turn in the trend of the market.

If the M.B.I. is to be of any use it must be of use *now*, and not by way of that most accurate and least powerful of all instruments, the retrospectroscope, the machine that looks backward with great precision. Well, certain conclusions can

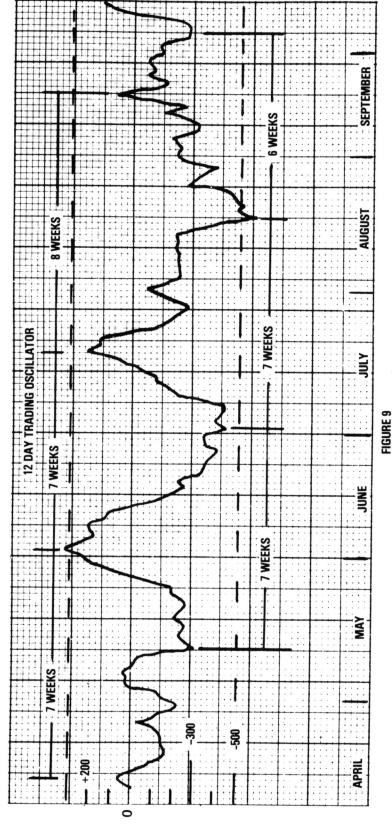

FIGURE 9

THE PERIODICITY OF APPEL'S 12 DAY TRADING OSCILLATOR

82

indeed be drawn. Zones 5 and 1 are visited only briefly. In a bear market, readings over 60 are not maintained for long periods and the same applies to those under 21. Patience, therefore, in waiting for such readings should be rewarded. Zones 4 and 2 are the normal reversal zones and for an active trader, waiting for these zones should show reasonable profit. The idea was to *define and avoid trading* in Zone 3 (except for some special spread plays), even though the short term trend was well defined. This is because the distance from Zone 3 to either Zone 5 or Zone 1 is obviously much shorter than the distance from either Zone 5 or Zone 1 to the opposite zone. And Figure 7 clearly shows that the M.B.I. can go directly and without hesitation from Zone 5 to Zone 1, and vice versa.

This is how I derived my indicator. It gives me a number for each day that I calculate it and the great thing about numbers is that they are nonemotional and they give a feeling of security and tranquility. When the indicator is in overbought territory and my friends are chasing stocks, I can sit back and relax and let the market come back to me. They may make some money while I do nothing or go short, but in the long run my performance will be better than theirs' as I will be playing the percentages. One of the great ways to do that is via option trading, totally modernized by the Chicago Board of Options Exchange; indeed so successful that the American Exchange joined forces in January 1975 to form the Options Clearing Corporation.

CHAPTER 7

OPTIONS TRADING
REVOLUTIONIZED BY THE
CHICAGO BOARD OPTIONS EXCHANGE

Chapter 7

Options Trading Revolutionized By The Chicago Board Options Exchange

An option is a contract, on the part of the *writer* of the contract, to deliver (in the case of a "call"), or receive (in the case of a "put"), stock at a predetermined price, called the Strike Price, up to a predetermined date, expiration date. The C.B.O.E., at this time of writing, deals only in CALL contracts so our attention will be focused on them, but there are plans to deal in PUT contracts in the future, so it is good to know something about them also.

An option contract is a dealing between individual investors—one investor writes, "sells", the contract to another who buys it. Let us imagine I own *100 shares of stock* at 40. (*Cost of stock and price of option* are usually given on a *per share* basis). I am thinking of selling it on the open market, but instead of selling them outright at 40, their present price, I might consider writing a call on them at 40, and thereby receive a premium of about 10% for a 6 month 10 day contract. (Shorter contracts command less premium because, like a warrant, an option is a wasting asset and the premium diminishes during the life of the option to disappear altogether on the expiration date). Let us say that with the stock I own at 40 ($40 per share), the call might be purchased from me for 5 ($5 per share). This means that for $5 the buyer of the call acquires the right to *buy from me* one share of stock at $40 per share at any time up to the expiration date. These transactions deal only in round lots of 100 shares—i.e., he would have to pay me $500 for the right to acquire 100 shares of stock at 40. Obviously, if the stock rises to 60 at expiration date, he can *CALL* it from me at 40, turn around and sell it on the open market at 60 and make 20 points, less what he paid me for the call (5 points), leaving 15 points profit. His profit is, therefore, $15 \div 4 \times 100\% = 375\%$. This is a good example of leverage and explains why a market player would want to buy a call. Notice, the buyer will lose his total stake ($500) if the stock is at 40 or below on expiration date, as the call would be worthless. (Clearly, there is no point in calling the stock from me at 40 when he can buy it in the open market for 35). However, though he loses his total stake of $500 *this is the maximum he can lose.* He knows, in advance, his total liability.

What about me, the writer of the call, what happens to me, and what advantage do I receive for selling the call? Well, if the stock is called from me at 40, I receive, in effect, 45 for it, $40 + 5$ (received from the call buyer). Since I was thinking of selling it at 40 originally, the fact that I have written a call on it has increased what I receive. But this is *all* I can receive. If the stock goes to 80, it still will be called from me at 40 and I still make just the 5 points.

If the stock falls to 35, the call expires worthless and I keep the 5 points so now I have an even position—i.e., I have acquired 5 points of downside protection. Only if the stock falls below 35 do I start to lose money by not having sold the stock outright at 40.

Notice the 6 month 10 day period mentioned earlier. This was for tax purposes, as capital gain changes from short-term to long-term after 6 months. Before the Chicago Board Options Exchange (CBOE) came into being, options were traded on an over-the-counter basis and individually negotiated, with the strike price being at, or very close to, the current market price of the underlying security. The buyer and the seller of the call were also pretty much locked in to each other for the life of the contract. That is to say that, if the purchaser of a call for some reason wanted to sell it before expiration date, he often had a hard time finding someone to buy it from him. In other words, there was not much of a secondary market, either for the option buyer or for the seller, if for some reason he wished to get out of his side of the contract. This sort of option trading has been going on for a long time, but not, I believe, in great volume because of the lack of a secondary market and the fact that the strike price had to be adjusted for dividends received by the writer. Also because the small investor was not encouraged to enter it.

However, the CBOE came up with some great ideas. What they did was:

1) Concentrated on a relatively small group of strong stocks actively traded on the Big Board. Call options are being added on an ongoing basis on both the CBOE and Amex. At the time I really started getting interested in options, the CBOE dealt in options on 32 stocks: (see Table VIII).

2) Standardized the expiration date to the last trading Monday of the month after which the options are named—an October 1975 option on Pennzoil (or any other stock) expires on the last trading Monday of October 1975 and trading ceases the preceding Friday. Presently, options expire in January, April, July and October. And the new series in August, November, February and May.

3) Standardized strike prices; to the nearest 20 points on high-priced stocks such as I.B.M., nearest 10 on most stocks and for the low priced stocks the nearest 5 points. This is just an example, but it is possible that if a stock had had a large up (or down) move, 4 or 5 October 1975 options of different strike price might be traded. Lets call the stock ZYX. We might have an October 1975 *60* ZYX, meaning the strike price would be 60. This would have come into being at the end of January, when the January options expired. However, if the stock fell to 50, an October *50* on ZYX would be issued by the CBOE and an October *40* if the stock fell to 40. If the stock still kept on going down the strike prices might now become 5 points apart—i.e. there might be an October *35* ZYX. The CBOE decides and acts as a clearinghouse for buyers and sellers.

Actually, in 1974, with its disastrous mid-year action, multiple strikes were usual. For instance, the following POLAROID, January 1975 options, actually existed:

PRD Jan 1975 *60*
     Jan 1975 *45*
     Jan 1975 *40*
     Jan 1975 *35*
     Jan 1975 *30*
     Jan 1975 *25*
     Jan 1975 *20*
     Jan 1975 *15*

This gives rise to the possibility of "spread trading," which will be described later.

4) The CBOE also eliminated any adjustment of the strike-price for dividends received by the writer of the call. He who owns the stock keeps the dividends.

At this point it might be useful to examine the similarities and differences between CBOE options and warrants.

CBOE OPTION	**WARRANT**
1. Written by individual investor CBOE acts as clearinghouse.	Written by parent corporation.
2. Short expiration period, no extension possible.	Long expiration period when originally written. May be extended by Corporation.
3. Multiple options issued by CBOE as stock price fluctuates.	Exercise price fixed by Corp. under original terms. Sometimes there are provisions for increasing E.P. after a certain date, but not usually for lowering it.
4. Premium relates to investor optimism.	Premium relates to investor optimism.
5. No dividends paid.	No dividends paid.
6. Purchase of call option an inexpensive way to "control" parent stock (leverage).	Purchase of warrant an inexpensive way to "control" parent stock (leverage).
7. Purchaser's liability limited to price paid for option.	Purchaser's liability limited to price paid for warrant.
8. Option premiums are received immediately by holder of parent stock.	Warrant premiums can only be captured by selling them short.
9. Can be sold on a declining stock without an "uptick". (See Appendix)	Can only be shorted on an "uptick"
10. Margin requirements unfavorable for naked option writing.	Margin requirements unfavorable for low-priced warrants.

Options usually have some *premium*. That is value over intrinsic value. Options nearing expiration date may actually be selling below their intrinsic value—not much below, of course, or the arbitrageurs would buy and exercise them. The premium depends on many factors—such as state of market, price and volatility of parent stock, strike price of option, investor psychology and the length of time the option still has to run. An option that is *all* premium is an *out-of-the-money option*. For instance, an October *50* ZYX might have gone for 4.8 (4 7/8) when ZYX was trading at 47. Obviously, such an option has no intrinsic value, as the stock is below the strike price—i.e. it's out of the money. However, the October *45* ZYX might be priced at 7.1 (7 1/8). This is *in the money* 2 points (47 less 45, the strike price), the remaining 5.1 points being premium. This is an *in-the-money option*, as it has 2 points *of intrinsic value*.

Let us examine a typical CBOE trade. Investor A owns 100 shares of stock ZYX. He carries it in a margin account and when he writes a call on this stock, the money received is credited immediately to his margin account; his No. 2 account. (Note the *purchase* of CALLS cannot be margined even though the transaction may be carried in the No. 2 account—the margin account; and they have to be *sold* in the No. 2 account, the margin or the No. 3 account, the short account). Notice that if he buys stock *for the purpose of selling a call on this stock*, the price received for the call can be *applied towards the purchase of the stock*. Investor B, who buys the call, has to pay 100% of the cash price as the purchase cannot be margined. There is only one kind of buyer—you are a buyer and that's it—period. But there are *two* classes of sellers and it is important to know the difference. Investor A above, who has written a call on a *stock he owns* has written a *covered* option and he is a *covered writer*. However, it is possible for an investor to write an option on a stock he does *not* own, and has no intention of owning. Such an investor has written a "*naked*" option and he is a *naked writer*, subject to definite regulations. These vary somewhat between brokerage houses, but my house demands total equity in the account of over $10,000, with additional margin requirements against the naked sale. Those are: 40% of the market value of the stock, less the premium received, less points away (See Chap. 11). "Naked" transactions are carried in the "short" account, the No. 3 account.

The naked writer has sold the option short, in other words. Actually, that is also what the covered writer has done, but in his case the underlying stock he owns makes it possible for the transaction to be carried in his No. 2 account with the advantage to him that this account is not marked to the market in the way the No. 3 account is (see Chap. 11).

Selling short and the writing of "naked" options are widely regarded as highly risky procedures, but how risky are they, particularly how risky is the writing of naked options? Let us take a theoretical but imminently possible situation involving a notable and volatile stock, VOL. Presently, the stock is at 45. Investor A buys the stock and writes a covered call, expiring in 4 months, with a striking price of 45 and receives 5 points premium for the call, i.e., the cost for buying the stock is 45 minus 5 equals 40, ignoring commissions. What are the possibilities? If the stock at expiration date is 45, he makes 5 points (the price of the call). If the stock falls to 30, he has lost 15 points equity on the stock, gained 5 points on the call for a total loss of 10 points. (Note that, though the stock may recover, his equity has diminished 10 points no matter how he wants to describe it). If his stock rises to 60 and is called at 45, he makes 5 points. Writers of covered calls, as we have seen, do not profit greatly on large upside moves. Investor B writes a naked option under the same conditions, and he receives 5 points immediately. The possibilities are: the stock stays flat and expires at 45, so he gains 5 points. The stock falls to 30, he also receives the 5 points premium as the call will expire worthless. The stock rises to 60 and is called from him at 45. He now has to buy stock at 60 to deliver it to the buyer at 45. His loss is 60 minus 45 equals 15 points, less 5 points received for the call equals 10 points loss. There are, therefore, two differences between the writers of covered and of naked options:

1) The risks are on different sides of the market. The covered writer loses if the underlying stock goes down more than the call-price received. The naked writer loses if the underlying stock goes up and is called at a higher price than the striking price plus call price.

2) The naked writer has to accept his loss immediately because the stock is called on him, whereas the covered writer may hold for eventual recovery since he does not have to deliver if he is wrong. The risks of the naked writer, therefore, are more dramatic and somewhat greater, but remember, there is nothing to say that a stock held long may not just continue declining.

Naked option writing can give, and gave me in 1974, some dramatic gains. But if your Volatility Index is high, it is uncomfortable to carry a naked option in a No.

3 account, particularly now that the CBOE will not allow stop loss orders to be placed on options. I will have more to say about naked option writing, and other naked positions, "skinny-dipping" as I call it, when I discuss my Moving Balance System. In the meantime, just realize that if you go skinny-dipping you'd better remember where you left your clothes.

The writing of one covered option for 100 shares against 100 shares of stock owned is a form of hedging very similar to the stock long, warrants short 1:1 mix we have already discussed. Obviously, if you hope the stock will go up, but want significant downside protection, it is wise to write a call that is heavily *in-the-money* as this will give point for point received downside protection.
Example: Stock ZYX now 45
             October 25 ZYX option now 24

This option has 20 points intrinsic value (45-25) and 4 points premium. The stock can decline to 45 – 24 = 21 at expiration date before the overall position loses money as the 25 call will be worthless at any point 25 or below. If the stock rises, the investor gets his 4 points of premium no matter how high the stock goes. (Figure 10 compare with Figure 2). This is a good hedge, as a profit will be made anywhere above 21—i.e., if the stock is at 25 on expiration date the option is worthless.

At *25* therefore, the Sell Side will show the following profit (as the option will be worthless):

SELL SIDE

	Debit	Credit
October 25 option	0	2400
Profit = 24 points		

and the Buy Side the following loss:

BUY SIDE

	Debit	Credit
Stock ZYX	4500	2500
Loss = 20 points		

Overall profit = the 4 points of premium, already received.

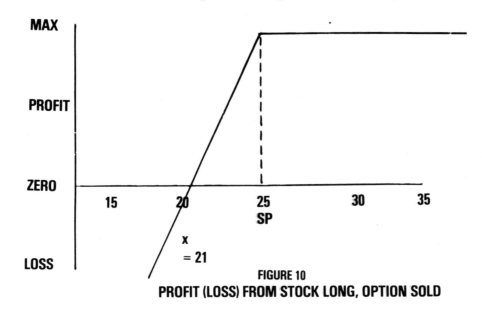

FIGURE 10
PROFIT (LOSS) FROM STOCK LONG, OPTION SOLD

Note this is all he receives if the stock is anywhere above 25. What he has gained is *downside protection.* If, on the other hand, the investor was bullish it would pay to write an *out-of-the-money* option as the profit potential on the upside would be greater.

ZYX presently 45

January *60* option presently 3

If ZYX rises to 60 at expiration date, the profit is 60 – 45 = 15 plus the 3 points received for the call = 18, as the call is worthless at 60 or anywhere below. Notice that if the writer decides to write a mix of options, say 3 options for 100 shares each against 100 shares held long, *1* of these options is a covered option and the other 2 are naked options and require margin. The formula for the upside breakeven point for the above situation is very similar to Formula 1 for warrants. It is Formula 3.

Formula 3 To find upside breakeven point ''B'' when stock long, options written.

Upside breakeven point = B   Strike price = SP

Stock price paid (per share) = SPP

Option price received (per share) = OPR

B – SPP = (B – (SP + OPR)) No. of options written

i.e. B – 45 = (B – (60 + 3)) 3

B – 45 = 3 B – 189

2 B = 144

B = 72

At *72*, therefore, the Buy Side will show the following profit:

BUY SIDE

	Debit	Credit
100 shares ZYX	4500	7200
Profit = <u>27 points</u>		

and the sell side the following loss (as each 60 option sold at 3 is now worth 72 – 60 = 12 points):

SELL SIDE

	Debit	Credit
Jan. 3 60 options	3600	900
each worth 12	(12 x 3)	(3 x 3)
Loss = <u>27 points</u>		

i.e. profit will be made on the upside until 72 when *loss* will occur at the rate of *2 points* (the naked options) *per each point rise in the parent stock.*

The downside protection in this situation is the stock price paid (45) less total option price received (9) = 36 (Figure 11). Such are examples of hedges of stock held long against options written. However, if an investor was really convinced that a stock was going to go down (for instance, market in Zone 5, stock acting

232

weakly—bad news about the company) he could short the stock but *buy* a call protecting himself thereby at a price on the upside if he was wrong in his predictions. An example:

ZYX presently at 50 and expected to tumble down, but upside protection needed against catastrophic loss.

		Debit	Credit
(a)	Sell short 100 shares ZYX		5000
(b)	Buy, Jan. 1, 50 ZYX option at 6	600	

If ZYX falls as planned—say to 30

At *30* therefore, the Sell Side will show the following profit:

SELL SIDE

	Debit	Credit
Profit = 20 points	3000	5000

and the Buy Side the following loss:

BUY SIDE

	Debit	Credit
(option will be worthless)	600	0

Loss = 6 points
Overall Profit = 14 points

If ZYX rises to 60

At *60*, therefore, the Buy Side will show the following profit:

BUY SIDE

	Debit	Credit
(a) (option is worth 10 60 – 50)	600	1000

Profit = 4 points

SELL SIDE

	Debit	Credit
(b) Loss = 10 points	6000	5000

Total loss = 10 − 4 = <u>6 points</u>

This will be the loss no matter how high the stock rises.

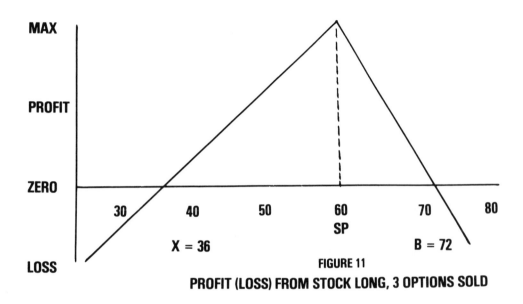

FIGURE 11

PROFIT (LOSS) FROM STOCK LONG, 3 OPTIONS SOLD

Occasionally, an interesting situation may occur when profit can be made on the upside in spite of a short sale of stock. On Monday, September 23, 1974, the Wall Street Journal gave details of an interesting play by none other than our old friend, Ed Thorp, of *Beat The Market*. (I just knew he had to be playing the CBOE).

Thorp follows the price action of options on his computer, which is programmed to detect unusual option prices. In this case with Upjohn (symbol UPJ) selling on June 11, 1974 at 88, the July 1974 *85* C.B.O.E. option was going for 5. Thus for $5 you could acquire the right to buy one share of UPJ for $85. The computer reckoned that the price should be 7.50—i.e. the options were underpriced. So what did Thorp do (he runs a fund so he has a bit of money to play with)? He:

SOLD SHORT

	Debit	Credit
3200 shares of UPJ at 88		281,600

and

BOUGHT

50 *85* UPJ options at 5	25,000	

(Note this controls 50 x 100 = 5000 shares).

Now, provided UPJ moved *one way or the other*, but *didn't stay still* a profit would be made on a move either way. First, the situation if the stock is at 85 (strike price) when the options expire.

At *85* therefore, the Sell Side will show the following profit:

SELL SIDE

	Debit	Credit
3200 UPJ sold short at 88 covered at 85	272,000	281,600

Profit = 96 points (3 x 32)

and the Buy Side the following loss:

BUY SIDE

	Debit	Credit
50 *85* options bought now worthless	25,000	0

Loss = 250 points

Overall loss = 154 points ($15,400.00)
This is the *maximum loss.*

However, as soon as UPJ *falls*, giving a profit of more than $25,000 (the cost of the options) the overall position will show a profit. The breakeven point is at 80.2, as there will be at that point a drop of 7.8 points x 3200 (shares sold short) = $25,000 profit, to be set against $25,000 loss on the options.

What about the upside point, because profit will *begin here* beyond a certain point as there are more shares controlled by the options (5000) than stock sold short? This point is given by Formula 4.

Formula 4 To find upside breakeven point "B" in unbalanced mix stock short, options bought.

$$\text{Upside breakeven point} = B$$

$$\text{Strike Price} = SP$$

$$\text{Stock Price received} = SPR$$

$$\text{Option price paid} = OPP$$

$$(B - (SP + OPP)) \text{ No. options bought}$$

$$= (B - SPR) \frac{\text{No. shares sold}}{100}$$

i.e.
$$(B - (85 + 5)) 50 = (B - 88) \frac{3200}{100}$$

$$50B - 4500 = 32B - 2816$$

$$18B = 4500 - 2816$$

$$18B = 1684$$

$$B = 93.6 \ (93.56)$$

At *93.6* therefore, the Buy Side will show the following profit:

BUY SIDE

	Debit	Credit
Stock at 93.6		
85 options are worth	25,000	43,000
93.6 − 85.0 = 8.6 x 50	(5 x 5000)	(8.6 x 5000)
Profit = <u>180 points</u>		

and the Sell Side the following loss:

SELL SIDE

	Debit	Credit
Loss = <u>180 points</u>	93.6 x 3200 = 299,600	88 x 3200 = 281,600

(The Sell Side figure has been adjusted slightly, and commissions have been ignored).

Notice in this situation when the upside breakeven point is reached the system will *develop* profit, as there are a greater number of shares controlled by the options than have been sold short (Figure 12). What actually happened was the stock fell to 75.5 and Thorp's fund made about $14,400 on the deal in less than 3 weeks, on a total investment of about $170,000 as the short sale required posting only 50% margin.

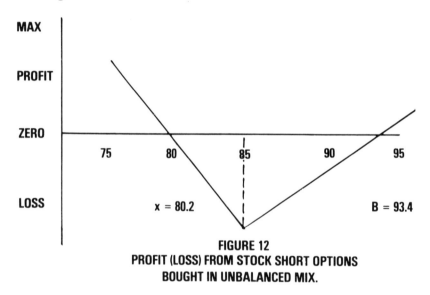

FIGURE 12
PROFIT (LOSS) FROM STOCK SHORT OPTIONS
BOUGHT IN UNBALANCED MIX.

There is one extremely positive and favorable aspect to CBOE option trading and that is that traders, both buyers and sellers, can liquidate their position *whenever they choose*, as there is an active secondary market. A buyer simply sells the call he has bought. And gain (loss) is counted as capital gain (loss) either short-term or long-term, depending on the length of time the position has been held.

The writer can annul his side of the contract by purchasing *as a closing transaction* an option identical (except for price, of course) to the one he wrote—i.e. if he *sold* a January 75 *35* PRD, he *buys* a January 75 *35* PRD as a closing transaction. In this situation, gain (loss) is treated as *ordinary income* gain (loss), and this has important income tax considerations which will be discussed in a later chapter.

Hedging, as used in this book, refers to the relationship between stock and options (or warrants), either stock long vs. options written (or warrants short) or stock short vs. options (or warrants) bought. However, because of the multiple strike prices of the CBOE options, a special type of hedging *that does not involve the parent stock at all* can be performed *involving options and options only*. This is called spreading or spread trading and it is the subject of the next chapter.

CHAPTER 8

SPREAD TRADING FOR PROFIT
AND PRESERVATION OF CAPITAL

Chapter 8

Spread Trading For Profit
And Preservation Of Capital

Thanks to the multiple strike prices that exist on the CBOE and Amex, marvelous opportunities occur for spread trading. I wish that at the time that I was devising my Moving Balance System, I had run across Harry Snyder's essays on spreading. Maybe nothing comes together all at once but what I can do now is acknowledge the effect his essays have had on me. Harry Snyder is co-manager of the option department of Herzog & Co., 170 Broadway, New York, N.Y. 10038.

Every time I thought about spreading, it seemed that another play would come to me. The possibilities are really incredible. And from my warrant-shorting days, I realized the great value of profit (loss) diagrams. They can give a real overview of the picture in a way that no series of figures can. And all a profit (loss) diagram needs are three values:

1) Point of maximum gain (or loss). This is without exception at the higher or lower strike price.

2) The downside breakeven point = X.

3) The upside breakeven point = B.

Since at the present time *calls* only are traded on the CBOE and Amex, the downside breakeven point can often be calculated in one's head for both spreads and hedges. For instance, if I purchase a stock for 50 and write a call or calls against it, my downside protection is not related to the number of calls I have written; only to the total amount I have received. One call written at 15 provides the same downside protection (at expiration date) as 3 calls written at 5 points each. The difference is *only* at the point at which one gets full protection. Obviously, if the options become worthless at a stock price above the breakeven point, the position will show a profit. However, downside loss—which is what we are considering—will start at the identical point. Notice that upside and downside breakeven points are related to prices at *expiration*—the same prices *before* expiration will *not* give the same profit-loss diagrams as the calls will probably still carry some premium over intrinsic value.

Since calls only are traded, there are more formulae in this book for finding B—the upside breakeven point, than there are for finding X—the downside breakeven point. Finding B in the situations we are going to consider cannot easily be done by mental arithmetic, so I have devised formulae for the various plays discussed. Since they vary in subtle ways, they are certainly not worth trying to remember. Also since what we are trying to find is a breakeven point—that point at which profit on one side balances loss on the other—the formula can be *seen* to work when the answer is found, by working out the profit and loss figures on the two sides. And they *have* to balance out. If they don't only three things are possible:

1) The math is wrong.

2) The wrong formula has been used.

3) The formula is wrong.

Formula 10 came into being because Formula 6 would not work and it took me a little time to figure out why it wouldn't. But I have found the proper formula for the situation, and if you discover (and I certainly hope you don't because I have checked them all out now) that a formula in a particular situation does not balance and you know that conditions (1) and (2) above do *not* obtain, then you can have the fun of devising your own formula. The point I am really trying to get across is that one needs a handle on all the different possibilities that may occur and I believe truly that profit (loss) diagrams with breakeven points are the way to do it.

Spread trading is entered into in the expectation of one of three possibilities occuring:

1) The stock (which is *not* purchased, remember, but on which the spread is based) declines in value. A spread expecting such action is a *bearish spread.*

2) The stock appreciates. A spread based on such an expectation is a *bullish spread.*

3) No strong convictions are held one way or the other about the final position of the parent stock on expiration, but a profit is desired whether the stock goes up *or* down. There are two main types of such a spread—the multiple neutral spread and what Harry Snyder calls the "butterfly" spread.

Let us consider a very simple spread—one that is bearish. Being bearish is fine but nobody wants to be up there without a paddle, so protection is needed. The idea is to be correct, but to be prepared to be less than spectacularly correct in exchange for not being catastrophically wrong. Please pick up the daily paper and look at the Chicago Board of Options Exchange column. As I write this I am looking at the figures for November 8, 1974, when the M.B.I. was high (58—see Figure 7). The market was, on the basis of the M.B.I. figures, at least primed for some sort of down move—i.e. this is *no* time to initiate a bullish spread. But a bearish spread might be very much in order. Looking at my paper, as you might look at yours for a similar situation, I scan the list of stocks to see if perhaps the following "set" occurs. What I am looking for is this: (1) a strike spread—that is, the difference between the strike prices of a pair of options—of 10 points with the difference between the prices of the options traded (at these strikes) not more than two or three points less than the *strike spread*. The difference between the prices of the options we will call the "basis"—a term I learned from Harry Snyder and a very good one. The strike spread we can refer to as S.S.

Let's assume it's early November 1974, and we favor a bearish spread. The newspapers indicate that there are a number of attractive possibilities, but let's pick McDonald's (MCD), as the stock is volatile.

Here we go:

		Jan.	Apr.	July	MCD Stock
MCD	60	3/8	b	b	38-3/4
	50	1-3/4	b	b	
	40	4-1/4	6-3/8	b	
	35	6-3/8	8-1/2	10	
	30	10-1/4	12	13-1/2	
	25	14-3/8	15-3/4	b	

b = no option offered.

This stock is at 38.7 (decimals are much to be preferred to fractions*), so one should concentrate on the options around that price. There are two, the MCD 40 and the MCD 35. An interesting bearish spread could be initiated as follows:

Sell   1 MCD Apr. *25* receive 15.7

Buy   1 MCD Apr. *35* pay 8.5

Here the *strike spread* is 35 – 25 = 10. The *basis* is 15.7 – 8.5 = 7.2. Just looking at these figures I know the possible loss (if the stock rises) is 10 – 7.2 = *2.8*, versus the possible gain (if the stock drops to 25) of *7.2*—i.e. 7.2 ÷ 2.8 = 2.5 ratio of reward to risk if I am right. How come? How can I look at the paper and say to my wife (or to anyone else with her gift for listening), "There's an interesting bearish spread on McDonald's April options. Profit possibility 7.2, against possible loss of 2.8."

Well it's really very simple. Let us examine the situation if MCD declines to zero. Clearly, both options will be worthless—i.e.,

---

*1/8 = 0.08, 1/4 = 0.2, 3/8 = 0.4, 1/2 = 0.5, 5/8 = 0.6, 3/4 = 0.7, 7/8 = 0.8.

At *O* therefore, the Sell Side will show the following profit:

SELL SIDE

	Debit	Credit
Sell one MCD Apr. 25	0	1570

Profit = <u>15.7 points</u>

and the Buy Side the following loss:

BUY SIDE

	Debit	Credit
Buy one MCD Apr. 25	850	0

Loss = 8.5 points

Profit = 15.7 – 8.5

$\qquad$ = <u>7.2 points</u>

$\qquad$ = "The Basis."

MCD rises to 100—what happens? No sweat.

At *100* therefore, the Buy Side will show the following profit:

BUY SIDE

	Debit	Credit
Buy 1 MCD Apr. 35 at 100, option will be worth 100 – 35 = 65	850	6500

Profit = 65.0 – 8.5 = <u>56.5 points</u>

and the Sell Side the following loss:

SELL SIDE

	Debit	Credit
Sell 1 MCD Apr. 25 at 100	7500	1570

option will be worth
100 – 25 = 75

Loss = 75.0 – 15.7 = <u>59.3 points</u>

Overall loss 59.3 – 56.5 = <u>2.8 points</u>

A one to one *bearish* spread like this will *always* fulfill the following conditions.

A 1:1 Bearish spread

Maximum profit = The basis

To remind you—this is the difference between the actual prices of the two options.

Maximum loss = strike spread minus basis

To return to the table of MCD, obviously the 40 - 30 pair would be an inferior choice as:

Sell 1 MCD Apr *30* receive 12.0

Buy 1 MCD Apr *40* pay 6.4

Strike spread = 10

Basis = 5.6

Maximum profit = *5.6*

Maximum loss = 10 – 5.6 = *4.4*

Notice, of course, this discussion is for one option sold vs. one option bought, but the same relationship will apply for any 1:1 proportion. For 10 options sold vs. 10 options bought, everything will be multiplied by 10, *that is all*.

I believe most people imagine the market to be a good deal more difficult than it actually is. As I have said, I do not claim to be any kind of a market financial expert. I do not really understand such things as the flow of money, gold reserve, dollar value abroad, and all the other things that have an effect on the market, and I never try to predict what effect any particular piece of news will have on the market. I am quite prepared to see how the market responds because it will do so more or less in time with the M.B.I. I could mention the recent coal strike. The reason that it may be significant just now is that the market is primed to go down and "needs" a reason to do so. Actually, I am at the moment happy with any action of the market—because of my heavily hedged position. I will follow my indicators daily and, while the market decides where it wants to go, I will be devoting all the time I can to this book because although I really know nothing about finances, I *do* claim to be in tune with the market via my Moving Balance Indicator, and I *do* claim to understand hedging and spreading.

To return to the bearish spread, we were considering the MCD 35/25.

Sell 1 MCD Apr *25* receive 15.7.

Buy 1 MCD Apr *35* pay 8.5.

We have seen that if the stock rises, the maximum loss is 2.8, and if it falls to zero the gain will be 7.2. Where is the point at which the maximum gain of 7.2 is achieved? Obviously, it will be at that point where both options are worthless. This is the *lower strike price* = 25. At this point, the amount received for a now worthless option is 7.2 points more than the amount paid for a now worthless option. This brings out an important concept in spreading; the maximum gain in any spread will be related, depending on the type of spread, to either the higher or the lower strike price. Since maximum profit is at 25 or below, where is the upside breakeven point above 25? (Total possible loss is only 2.8, remember, but at some point there will be a balance). This is given by Formula 5.

Formula 5   To find upside breakeven point "B" for 1:1 bearish spread:

111

Upside breakeven point   = B (Upside is used to denote "above lower strike")

Lower strike   = LS

Amount received (per option) = AR

Amount paid (per option)   = AP

$AR - (B - LS) = AP$

$15.7 - 8.5 = B - 25$

$25 + 15.7 - 8.5 = B$

$B = 32.2$

At *32.2* therefore, the Sell Side will show the following profit (each 25 option will be worth 7.2):

SELL SIDE

	Debit	Credit
1 MCD 25 is worth 32.2 – 25.0 = 7.2	720	1570
Profit = <u>8.5 points</u>		

and the Buy Side the following loss:

BUY SIDE

	Debit	Credit
1 MCD 35 will be worthless	850	0
Loss = <u>8.5 points</u> = position even.		

A more bearish spread. What about a more bearish spread? For instance, how about selling *2* lower priced options and buying *1* higher priced option. Let us consider the same options:

MCD

	Debit	Credit
Sell 2 MCD Apr. 25		3140
		(15.7 x 2)
Buy 1 MCD Apr. 35	850	

The maximum profit will be again at that point where both options are worthless—the lower strike—and will be 31.4 – 8.5 = *22.9 points*. This can be found by mental arithmetic. There will be, however, an upside breakeven point *beyond which loss will occur*, increasing point for point with any rise in value of the common. Formula 6 gives the upside breakeven point for a multiple bearish spread. The symbols are the same as in Formula 5, with the addition of the higher strike (HS).

Formula 6 (also see Formula 10) To find "B" for multiple bearish spread.

$$(AR - (B - LS)) \text{ number calls sold}$$

$$= (AP - (B - HS)) \text{ number calls bought}$$

our example:

$$(15.7 - (B - 25)) 2 = 8.5 - (B - 35) 1$$
$$31.4 - (2B - 50) = 8.5 - (B - 35)$$
$$31.4 - 8.5 = (2B - 50) - (B - 35)$$
$$22.9 = 2B - 50$$
$$= \underline{B - 35}$$
$$= B - 15$$
$$22.9 + 15 = B$$
$$B = \underline{37.9}$$

At *37.9* therefore, the Sell Side will show the following profit (as each 25 option will be worth 12.9):

SELL SIDE

	Debit	Credit
Sell 2 MCD 25	2580	3140
each will be worth	(12.9 x 2)	(15.7 x 2)
37.9 – 25 = 12.9		
Profit = <u>5.6 points</u>		

and the Buy Side the following loss:

BUY SIDE

	Debit	Credit
Buy 1 MCD 35		
each 35 MCD will be worth		
37.9 – 35 = 2.9	850	290
Loss = <u>5.6 points</u>		

Notice above this point, 37.9, the position will lose point for point with the common as the common rises because one of the options sold will be "unprotected." (The other will be protected by the option bought). The geometric profit picture given in Figure 13.

There are two basic bearish spreads, therefore:

1) A 1:1 bearish spread. The profit (loss) potential of which can be worked out easily by mental arithmetic.

2) A mix involving more lower strike options sold than higher strike options bought.

Bearish spreading should obviously only be undertaken in the expectation of a market decline; i.e., the market should be in Zones 4 or 5.

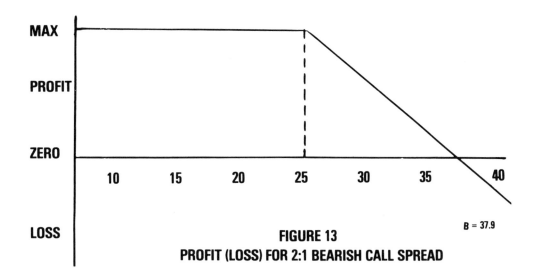

FIGURE 13
PROFIT (LOSS) FOR 2:1 BEARISH CALL SPREAD

What about bullish spreads?

A 1:1 bullish spread is the exact opposite of a 1:1 bearish spread. To consider the McDonalds options again, let us take the same pair of options except that in a bullish spread *one buys the lower strike and sells the higher strike.* i.e.,

Buy 1 MCD Apr *25* pay 15.7

Sell 1 MCD Apr *35* receive 8.5.

(This play is given for example only, as the profit-loss potential makes it undesirable). The strike spread is again 35 – 25 = 10 and the basis (the difference between the option prices) is again 15.7 – 8.5 = 7.2. A bullish spread is undertaken in the expectation of an advance. Let's imagine that at expiration date the stock is 50. What would the situation be?

At *50* therefore, the Buy Side will show the following profit (as each 25 option is now worth 25):

BUY SIDE

	Debit	Credit
1 MCD Apr. 25 worth 50 – 25 = 25	1570	2500
Profit = <u>9.3 points</u>		

and the Sell Side the following loss (as each 35 option is now worth 15):

SELL SIDE

	Debit	Credit
1 MCD Apr. 35		
worth 50 – 35 = 15	1500	850
Loss = 6.5 points		
Overall profit = 9.3 – 6.5 points		
= 2.8 points		

This is the strike spread minus the basis.

10 – 7.2 = 2.8

Imagine the downside picture:

At 25 or below both options will be worthless. The loss will, therefore, be the difference between the amount paid for the lower strike option and the amount received for that of the higher strike. Lo and behold—this is *the basis*. We can summarize the situation as follows:

	Max. Profit	Max. Loss
1:1 bearish spread	basis	S.S. – basis
1:1 bullish spread	S.S. – basis	basis

1:1 bullish spreads with calls often do not have enough profit potential, when the M.B.I. is low, to make them worthwhile. If you really have the courage of your bullish convictions, a 2:1 bullish spread will provide a good profit if you are correct. (But far too big a loss if incorrect). For example:

BUY

	Debit	Credit
2 MCD Apr. 25	3140	
	(15.7 x 2)	

SELL

1 MCD Apr. 35		850

at the same points 50 and 25—the situation is as follows:

At *50* therefore, the Buy Side will show the following profit (as each 25 option will be worth 25):

BUY SIDE

	Debit	Credit
2 Apr. 25	3140	5000
		(25 x 2)

Profit = <u>18.6 points</u>

and the Sell Side the following loss (as the 35 option will be worth 15):

SELL SIDE

	Debit	Credit
1 Apr. 35	1500	850

Loss = 6.5 points

Overall profit = 18.6 – 6.5
                   = <u>12.1 points</u>

However, for this gain the loss potential at 25, when all options would be worthless (i.e., 31.4 – 8.5 = 22.9 points) would have been risked. This is a profit/loss ratio of *un*acceptable proportions:

12.1 ÷ 22.9 = 0.53.

Actually, a bullish spread with puts (if and when they are traded on the CBOE and Amex) would be greatly preferred to this situation (see Chapter 12).

Once a bull market is underway, there is a safe bullish play that is worth knowing about. As an example, February 1975 represented a strong market period in the early phase of the bull market that started in late 1974. At that time, Burrough's (BGH) July 75 options, (stock at 81) had the following values:

BURROUGHS OPTIONS	PRICE
July 80	8.5
July 70	14.0
July 60	20.0

The first thing apparent in the above is that the July 60 was selling under its intrinsic value. Clearly, if the parent stock sells for 81 it ought to be worth at least 21 (60 + 21 = 81). Notice that although arbitrage is theoretically possible here, the commissions take away any profit. If a lynx-eyed, well-heeled investor should buy a number of July 60 options at 20 and convert them into stock, his purchase price would be 80 for a stock valued in the market place at 81. If he then sold the stock he would make an easy profit. Alas, all he would do actually is make his broker rich.

The July 70 option sells for 14—this has 11 points intrinsic value (81 – 70) and 3 points premium. But a very safe "bullish" play is possible as follows:

BUY

	Debit	Credit
10 BGH July 60's	20,000	
SELL		
10 BGH July 70's		14,000

(The new margin regulations—Chapter 11—do not put this play out-of-sight). If Burrough's closes at 70 *or at any point above 70* at the end of July, the profit will be as follows:

At *70* therefore, the Sell Side will show the following profit (as the options are worthless):

SELL SIDE

	Debit	Credit
Options are worthless	0	14,000
Profit = 140 points		

and the Buy Side the following loss:

BUY SIDE

	Debit	Credit
July 60 are worth 10	20,000	10,000
(70 – 60)		
Loss = 100 points		
Overall profit = 40 points		

This equals the strike spread less the basis: 10 – 6 = 4 times the number of options in spread

$$= 40$$

i.e., Burroughs can climb anywhere and you can make 40 points (on 10 options – 4 points per option). Or it can fall to 70, which is a 13.6% drop and you still make 4 points per option.* Maximum loss, which is the basis, occurs only at 60 and is 6 points times the number of options in spread. The downside breakeven point is given by Formula 7.

Formula 7   To find downside breakeven point "X" in a 1:1 bullish spread.

Downside breakeven point	= X
Lower strike	= LS
Amount paid per option	= AP
Amount received per option	= AR

$$X = LS + (AP - AR)$$

$$= 60 + (20 - 14)$$

$$= 66.$$

At *66* therefore, the Sell Side will show the following profit:

SELL SIDE

	Debit	Credit
Each 70 option will be worthless	0	14,000
Profit = <u>140 points</u>		

and the Buy Side the following loss:

---

*The tax situation is more favorable if the stock rises than if it falls to 70.

BUY SIDE

	Debit	Credit
Each 60 will be worth 6	20,000	6,000
(66 – 60)		

Loss = <u>140 points</u>

i.e., Burroughs can fall to 66, a fall of 18.5%, before money is lost.

For those who wish to be more bullish, for instance, buy 2 Jul 60's, and sell 1 Jul 70 in a situation like this (which I do *not* recommend as the M.B.I. on February 7, 1975 was 76), the downside breakeven point "X" is given by Formula 8. Symbols as in Formula 7 with the addition of the higher strike (H.S.).

Formula 8* To find "X" in multiple bullish spread.

$$(AP - (X - LS)) \text{ number calls bought}$$

$$= (AR - (X - HS)) \text{ number calls sold}$$

in the Burroughs situation, above, "X" would be 76, derived as follows:

i.e., $(20 - (X - 60)) \, 2 = 14 - (X - 70)$

$40 - (2X - 120) = 14 - (X - 70)$

$40 - 14 = (2X - 120) - (X - 70)$

$26 = X - 50$

$X = 76$

---

*In a multiple bullish spread, with low priced options, when X is below the higher strike, the following formula should be used: TAP – (X – LS) number calls bought = TAR. Compare with Formula 10 for multiple bearish spreads.

At *76* therefore, the Sell Side will show the following profit:

SELL SIDE

	Debit	Credit
Each 70 is worth 6	600	1400
Profit = <u>8 points</u>		

and the Buy Side the following loss:

BUY SIDE

	Debit	Credit
Each 60 is worth 16	4000	3200
	(20 x 2)	(16 x 2)
Loss = <u>8 points</u>		

An amusing combination spread, well-named a butterfly spread by Snyder, is possible by combining a 1:1 bearish spread with a 1:1 bullish spread. If we consider, for simplicity, 1:1 bearish and 1:1 bullish spreads similar (except for the strike prices) to those already worked out individually for McDonalds options, the butterfly spread on the 35, 30, 25 options works out as follows:

<u>OPTIONS</u>	<u>PRICE</u>
Apr. 35	8.5
Apr. 30	12.0
Apr. 25	15.7

BUTTERFLY SPREAD

	Debit	Credit
Buy 1 Apr. 35	850	
Sell 2 Apr. 30		2400
		(12 x 2)
Buy 1 Apr. 25	1570	

This is merely a combination of:

(1) A 1:1 BEARISH SPREAD

	Debit	Credit
Buy 1 Apr. 35	850	
Sell 1 Apr. 30		1200

We have already seen why the maximum *profit* is the basis:

$$12 - 8.5 = 3.5$$

and the maximum *loss* is the strike spread less the basis:

$$5 - 3.5 = 1.5$$

and:

(2) A 1:1 BULLISH SPREAD

	Debit	Credit
Buy 1 Apr. 25	1570	
Sell 1 Apr. 30		1200

We have also seen why the maximum *profit* is the strike spread less the basis:

$$5 - (15.7 - 12.0) = 1.3 \text{ points}$$

and the maximum *loss* is the basis:

$$15.7 - 12.0 \qquad = 3.7 \text{ points}$$

On both sides of the spread the maximum profit is at 30.

At *30* therefore:

the bearish side will show a profit of 3.5

and the bullish side a profit of 1.3

total profit   = *4.8* points

The maximum possible loss *on the downside* will be:

bullish loss minus bearish gain = 3.7 - 3.5 = *0.2* points

and the maximum possible loss *on the upside* will be:

bearish loss minus bullish gain $= 1.5 - 1.3 = 0.2$ points.

The play is balanced therefore. Hence the name butterfly. This is a safe play. But note the stock needs to be very close to 30, the point of maximum profit on expiration date, for a reasonably good return to be achieved. The margin required will be *the possible loss on both sides*:

i.e., $1.5 + 3.7 = 5.2$ points

Important caution.

Spreading is fun, but it is very important to realize that the CBOE does not give (as far as I can tell) any kind of preferential treatment to spreads, and if they call the sell side on you not only do you have to pay two extra commissions (the purchase and sale of the underlying stock), but you also lose the spread.

Another type of bullish spread is possible as follows:

1) Sell an option of a near expiration date.

2) Buy an option of a far expiration date *at the same strike*.

This is a calendar spread (or horizontal spread) but in order to make money with this technique, the spreader must be *near* term bearish and long-term bullish. Therefore, this is not a primarily bullish spread. A primarily bullish spread should be based on the idea that the stock will act bullish immediately—i.e., the position should be taken in Zones 1, or 2, and that, from date of inception of the hedge, the trend will be up. What happens for the hedge just given? Let's take the MCD options again. For instance, the only option on the table with Jan., Apr., and July figures quoted is the MCD 30 which goes for 10.1 in Jan., 12.0 in Apr., and 13.5 in July.

What happens if we:

1) Sell 1 Jan *30* receive 10.1

2) Buy 1 Jul *30* pay 13.5

and the stock *acts bullish*, so that at the end of January the stock is, say, 45. The situation is this.

At *45* therefore:

BUY SIDE

	Debit	Credit
Stock at 45		
July option is worth	1350	1850
45 – 30 = 15 plus some		
premium, say, 3.5 = 18.5		
Profit = <u>5.0 points</u>		

SELL SIDE

	Debit	Credit
Stock at 45		
Jan. option is worth		
45 – 30 = 15	1500	1010
Loss = 4.9 points		
Overall profit = <u>0.1 point</u>		

What kind of bullish spread is that? Obviously, money will only be made if:

a) The stock declines so that the Jan 30 terminates with a profit.

5) The *now-unprotected* Jul call appreciates in value.

My advice—avoid such hedges unless you have good reason to be near-term bearish, long-term bullish.

There is another spread to consider for price appreciation, a *multiple neutral spread*, aimed at a price for the stock, on expiration date of the options, as close to the higher strike as possible. The idea is to:

1) Sell a larger number of *higher* priced strikes.

2) Buy a lesser number of *lower* priced strikes.

Depending on the expectations of the spreader, the situation can be set up to yield a profit even if the stock falls to zero. Notice that, here also, the parent stock is *not* bought. However, the outcome of the spread obviously depends on its action.

Let's think big and set up a multiple spread with I.B.M. Let us allocate the following prices to a pair of I.B.M. options:

I.B.M. Options	Price
I.B.M. Apr 220	7.4
I.B.M. Apr 200	11.5

These prices would occur when I.B.M. is trading around 160 to 175, with about 4 or 5 months to go before expiration of the options. But suppose the market was oversold. Could a spread be set up that would fulfill the following criteria?

a) Show a profit at expiration following a large downside move of the parent stock?

b) Show a profit from a large upside move?

Well, it is possible by a mix of 5 I.B.M.'s 220 sold to 2 I.B.M.'s 200 bought to show a profit if I.B.M. closes at the end of April anywhere between *0 and 238*. How large is large?

Let us examine the situation in detail.

Sell 5 I.B.M.'s Apr 220 for 7.4 each

Buy 2 I.B.M.'s Apr 200 for 11.5 each

AR = amount received per call

   = 7.4

Total amount received 7.4 x 5 = *37.0* points

AP = amount paid per call = 11.5

Total amount paid = 11.5 x 2 = *23.0* points

If I.B.M. falls to zero, both calls will be worthless (indeed they will both be worthless at any point under the lower strike of 200)—i.e., the downside profit will be 37.0 – 23.0 = *14.0* points. The largest profit will be made at the higher strike. If I.B.M. is exactly at 220 at expiration date, the 5 calls will be worthless = 37.0 points profit.

But also:

The 200 call will be worth 220 – 200 = 20

BUY SIDE

	Debit	Credit
2 200 Apr. I.B.M.'s	2300	4000
	(11.5 x 2)	(20 x 2)

Profit = 17.0 points

Total Profit = 37.0 + 17.0

         = 54 points

If the stock stays still or goes down we make 14, if it rises to 220 we make 54, but, of course, there is an upside breakeven point. Where is that? In multiple strikes on high priced securities it is easier to consider *the distance above the higher strike* and work out what this will be, rather than deal in the large numbers involved when considering the actual strike prices themselves. This can be done because in this situation the maximum profit will always be given *exactly* at the higher strike price and the position will be progressively less profitable thereafter until the breakeven point is reached.

Let the distance (in points per share) from the higher strike to the breakeven point be D. Obviously, the *higher strike plus* D *will equal* the breakeven point. This is shown in Formula 9. The symbols are the same as in the other formulae with the addition of D, the unknown distance above HS (the higher strike) and SS (the strike spread).

Formula 9   To find upside breakeven point

$$B = HS + D$$

(D – AR) number calls written = (SS – AP + D) number calls bought

SELL SIDE
  Sell 5 IBM's Apr. 220 receive 7.4 each
BUY SIDE
  Buy 2 IBM's Apr. 220 pay 11.5 each

D is found as follows:

$$(D - 7.4)\,5 = (20 - 11.5 + D)\,2$$

$$5\,D - 37.0 = 17.0 + 2\,D$$

$$3\,D = 37.0 + 17.0$$

$$= 54$$

$$D = 18$$

Breakeven point therefore:

$$B = HS + D$$

$$= 220 + 18$$

$$= 238$$

At *238* therefore, the Buy Side will show the following profit:

BUY SIDE

	Debit	Credit
Each 200 option at 238 is worth 38	7600 (38 x 2)	2300 (11.5 x 2)
Profit = <u>53 points</u>		

and the Sell Side the following loss:

SELL SIDE

	Debit	Credit
Each 220 option at 238 is worth 18	9000 (18 x 5)	3700 (7.4 x 5)
Loss = <u>53 points</u>		

Above 238, since there are 3 unprotected calls, the position will lose *3* points for each point rise in the common. The situation is given geometrically in Figure 14.

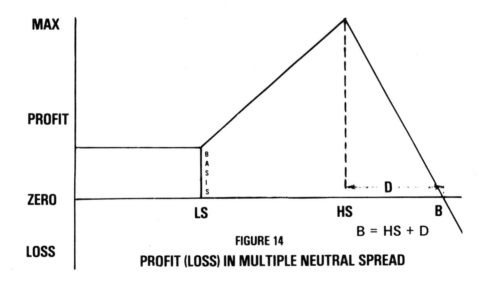

FIGURE 14
PROFIT (LOSS) IN MULTIPLE NEUTRAL SPREAD

There are also many other possibilities of spreading. For instance, the standard 1:1 bullish and 1:1 bearish spreads are *vertical* spreads in that they involve buying and selling different strike prices of *the same expiration date*. The play of selling a near-term option and buying a longer term option at the same strike is a *horizontal* spread. Obviously, these two techniques can be combined in all sorts of ways to provide *diagonal spreads* of varying degrees of steepness. But I feel that if you have followed me thus far, you will be able to enjoy working out such possibilities on your own. Spreading is great, as I have said, but please remember that most important caution—for to have the stock called and have the spread broken takes the frosting off the cake.

CHAPTER 9

HOW TO USE THE
MOVING BALANCE SYSTEM
ADVANTAGEOUSLY

Chapter 9

How To Use The
Moving Balance System Advantageously

I have said that the Moving Balance Indicator, on its own, can be used for timing stock purchases and sales. Table VIII gives the prices of some of the CBOE stocks at significant reversal points on the M.B.I. If your main interest is in buying stocks (or warrants or options), clearly you will improve your performance considerably if you buy on low M.B.I. readings and sell into high readings. I do not wish to give you the idea you will catch the exact reversal points of the market or of an individual stock. Indeed, if I had a system that could do that, I would keep it to myself, give up the practice of medicine and make a fortune for myself in the market.

The system I use, the Moving Balance System, is built on the idea that uncertainty is the only certainty. Playing the market is difficult for many reasons, one of the most important of which is that the market is ''out there'' doing its thing—whatever the latest exaggeration might be—while the player is sitting in his office looking down his microscope (or doing whatever his thing is). The player has to use a middleman and has to trust that middleman. But the player cannot really expect a baby-sitting service; which is why in the Moving Balance System the recommendation, particularly for those with a high volatility index, is to be hedged or spread and to hold no naked positions either *long* or *short*.

The system involves the following steps:

133

Step 1   Know your Volatility Index.

Please work it out now if you have not already done so. It is essential to know who you are and how you react. There is no shame attached to having a high Volatility Index—on the contrary, such people have a lot going for them in the world. But they do not have a lot going for them in the market. Characteristically, people of high Volatility Index "plunge"—I should know. A hot tip and, bang—out comes the check book. It is curious that whereas the decision to buy brand "a" over brand "b" in a department store is often carefully weighted, even by those with high Volatility Index, the much more important decision of stock selection is often accorded only the most cursory soul-searching. To repeat: I believe *strongly* that people with a high Volatility Index should be *hedged* or *spread* completely or almost completely. They need to be protected from themselves. So do those of low Volatility Index, but for different reasons—they need to be protected from the danger of too *little* action. The beauty of *spreading* is that action is preselected by the fact that options expire at a given date and not even "Mr. Spock" will fail to take a logical profit when the failure to move on the profit side would cause loss on the overall position of a hedge or a spread.

What about "James Bond?" Well, he can certainly go skinny-dipping (he will anyway); but there is that very important point to remember. Most of us who play the market, do so once removed. There is no analogy to any other game. In golf, you are on the course (no matter how much you would on occasion like to be elsewhere) while playing. In chess, you face the board and the pieces. In tiddlywinks, but why go on? You understand what I am driving at, because in the market *unless you are actually watching the tape*, you are really playing *in absentia.* Your broker is playing for you. He is also playing for all his other clients and what he really likes is the commodities market anyway. Under these conditions, why risk capital in a naked situation? In my opinion it is lunacy to take a naked position and hold it through thick and thin. A general practitioner once said to me in great seriousness, "Humphrey, I don't buy stocks to sell them. In fact," he said, "I have never sold a stock!" He has been at it a long time. He is, I believe, overall ahead of the game, but this I attribute to rather canny stock selection on his part, plus the fact that he has been in the market for

35 years. (I am not knocking his success, but I know he could have done much better than he has). Well, to return to the James Bonds of this world, and there are not very many of them, I think that the best "naked" play is to go short when the market is *heavily* overbought. Under these conditions, some sort of correction is predictable, and remember stocks often go down at 2 or 3 times the speed of any but the most *unusual advances*. Even so, a protective stop loss buy order should be placed.

Step 2   Consult the Moving Balance Indicator.

The rules are:

a) When the market is in Zones 5 and 4, think *down*. (i.e., bearish)

b) When the market is in Zones 1 and 2, think *up*. (i.e., bullish)

c) When the market is in Zone 3, *think* but sit on your hands. *Do* nothing (with the possible exception of a multiple neutral or butterfly spread if you must have action).

Step 3   Make a map.

A map is a *market-action-plan*. It will guide you in the market and will give substance to your decisions. Obviously, any old scrap of paper will do for preliminary skirmishes into possible positions, but once you have zoned onto a likely prospect, make a map, keep it and consult it. A map should contain all the following information.

MAP

1) Date

2) Volatility Index

3) Present M.B.I. reading

4) Present Zone

5) State of market (express in your own words)

6) The play (check one)

   Skinny Dip
   Hedge
   Spread

7) Formula used

8) Upside breakeven point
   Downside breakeven point

9) Point of maximum profit

10) Profit potential

11) Loss potential

12) Profit/Loss ratio

13) Acceptable level of success

14) Plan of evasive action

15) Progress report

16) Outcome

All this information can be condensed to keep for future reference as follows:

MAP

Date	3/6/74	V.I. 50
M.B.I.	63	
Present zone	5	

State of market	very vulnerable on the downside
Play	
Skinny Dip	
Hedge	
Spread	2:1 bearish ARC (Atlantic Richfield)
ARC	
present stock price	101.7
OPT July 100	8.4
July 90	15.0

SELL

	Debit	Credit
2 July 90		3000

BUY

	Debit	Credit
1 July 100	840	

Upside breakeven point (Formula 6)

$$(15.0 - (B - 90))\,2 = 8.4 - (B - 100)$$
$$30 - (2B - 180) = 8.4 - (B - 100)$$
$$30 - 8.4 = (2B - 180) - (B - 100)$$
$$21.6 = B - 80$$
$$B = 101.6 \text{ (Note profit will be made at any point below 101.6)}.$$

At *101.6* therefore, the Sell Side will show the following profit:

SELL SIDE

	Debit	Credit
90 worth 101.6 – 90 = 11.6	2320	3000
	(11.6 x 2)	

Profit = <u>6.8 points</u>

and the Buy Side the following loss:

BUY SIDE

	Debit	Credit
100 worth 101.6 – 100 = 1.6	840	160

Loss = <u>6.8 points</u>

Point of maximum profit 90 (both options worthless)

Profit potential = 30 – 8.4 = 21.6

Loss potential = when over 101.6

Profit/Loss ratio varies with loss potential

Acceptable level of success = 50% of profit potential = 11 points

Plan of evasive action see Step 5

Progress report 3.29 (M.B.I. 21)   ARC 94.2
                    July 100   4.7
                    July 90   9.8
        Profit (15.0 – 9.8) 2 – (8.4 – 4.7) = 6.7 points
            7.12 (M.B.I. 30)   ARC 86.4
                    July 100   0.1
                    July 90   0.8
        Profit (15.0 – 0.8) 2 – (8.4 – 0.1) = 20.1 points

Outcome   Position closed on 7.12 as 93% of maximum profit
                   received and M.B.I. rising.

Step 4   Keep a log.

This is to keep track of the actual transactions—which should be entered as soon as the confirmation slips are received. The following data are required.

Option date and Strike price

Opening date of Transaction (O D)

Closing date of Transaction (C D)

Debit

Credit

Profit

Loss

Naked options should be *starred*

Figures should be boxed when the position has been closed.

The following is a sample set of transactions in 1974. These would have been entered in the log under a whole page devoted only to Polaroid (PRD) options.

O D	C D		DEBIT	CREDIT	PROFIT	LOSS
6.7	8.23	100 shares PRD	4182			
6.7	8.23	1 Jan 75 40 sold	46	825	779	
6.7	8.26	*2 Jan 75 40 sold	94	1657	1563	
8.26	11.6	2 Jan 75 25 bought	513	609	96	
11.6		1 Jul 75 25 sold		560		

This gives a bird's eye view of all the transactions. The boxes around the figures in debit and credit columns denote that the transactions are closed (the profit figures confirm this). As the above log stands, a mere glance shows that 100 shares of PRD are held long in the account and that presently one covered option at 25 is outstanding against these shares. There are five important points:

1) It is usually within the power of the seller to decide if he will let these shares be called at *25*, because he can always terminate the July *25* transaction and write a different call, if that seems like a good play. (Warning: the CBOE may call the stock some weeks before the expiration

date of the option, so a plan to buy a covering call may not be possible).

2) The debit and credit figures entered show the actual amounts *after* commissions so that if the stock is called from him at 25, he will receive about 24.6, so his profit will be 2460 + 779 + 1563 + 96 + 560 – 4182 = 1276.

3) He is protected to 4182 – 2998 = 1184, i.e., to a fall in market value of around 12 points, before the overall position shows a loss: i.e., PRD can decline to 28% of its original value and he still breaks even. Just consider for a moment the situation if he hadn't been playing the CBOE successfully. He would have lost 72% of his equity (many have lost more). Note the figure 2998 is what he has already received (779 + 1563 + 96 + 560).

4) Providing PRD doesn't disappear altogether, he can use the original 100 shares again and again—like the young Lady of Spain—as a base for a a great deal of "covered" writing activity—i.e., he can *trade options against stock held.*

Aside—   "There was a young Lady of Spain
           Who liked it; now and again
           Not just—now and again
           But *now*
           And again and again and again."

Note: Because of the commission structure it is better to trade against 200 shares of stock.

5) All the transactions shown could actually have been made at the prices illustrated and *all are in consonance with the M.B.I.* I have picked examples of superior portfolio management, but the M.B.I. tells it like it is. The player used the Moving Balance System and managerial skills (which we will discuss later), but the important point is that just average skill as a manager would have shown a profit, provided one's decisions were *based on the M.B.I.*

Step 5   *Have a Plan of Evasive Action*

This is included in Step 3, but it is so important to think out a course of action if the situation goes against one, that I give this a full step on its own. In the Atlantic Richfield (AR) situation just discussed, the stock was at the upside breakeven point when the spread was set up. What should be done in a situation like this? Well, the first thing to realize is that the M.B.I. indicated that the market was vulnerable on the downside so that, *over the short term*, any great rise in the price of ARC is unlikely. The second point is that the loss will be point for point with the common stock, as one of the calls is unprotected.

An evasive action plan should have the following format:
Immediate protective action. Cover naked option if stock on a *declining M.B.I.* hits 103. Loss will be about 2 points plus commissions. If the M.B.I. advances, the position can be held for the subsequent decline. Longer term protection: Follow price of stock in relation to the M.B.I. curve. Close out the position if:

a) Stock advances on a declining M.B.I.

b) A satisfactory profit has been made and the M.B.I. is low.

The only situation where an evasive action plan is unnecessary is in a 1:1 spread situation, either bullish or bearish, because there the maximum possible loss (and also the maximum possible profit) will be known before entering the position.

Obviously, the most important step is Step 3—making a map. What are the choices? In an *overbought* market—M.B.I. in Zones 4 or 5—possibilities on the short side should be entertained. If one has the patience to wait for those occasions when the M.B.I. gets above 60, playing the short side is often safer and more profitable, (except in the strongest bull markets), than playing the long side in very oversold territory. There are three ways of playing the short side. These are:

a) Skinny-dipping

b) Hedging

c) Spreading

and there are a number of plays possible in each group.

SHORT SIDE OF THE MARKET

a] Skinny-dipping

This is only for hardy souls like "James Bond." If your Volatility Index is high, I really do not think you should take a large unprotected position on the short side because of the strain involved. The idea is to *have fun* in the market as well as make some money, so plays have to be picked consonant with both objectives. However, here are the naked plays.

Play 1   Sell stock [or warrants] short.

This puts you at full risk if the market goes against you. For this reason, protective stops are strongly advised, indeed, are essential.

Play 2   Sell [write] naked options.

Since stops may no longer be accepted on the CBOE, this play cannot be protected in the same way that play 1 can. It can, however, be protected by a *buy* order on the stock on which the naked option has been written. If the buy order, which should be 2 or 3 points above the present price of the stock (but still permit some profit), is triggered, the net effect is to convert the naked option into a "covered" option. This does not give as much profit as writing a covered option initially would do, of course, and does not offer as much downside protection on the stock purchased. For this reason, some traders will prefer, if the naked option goes against them, to close out the position ("cover"it) by buying a similar option to the one sold (as a closing transaction) and take the loss. This is presently an ordinary income loss, by the way, so the government will underwrite part of it.

b] Hedging

There are three basic hedging plays.

Play 3   Sell calls against stock held long.

Obviously, in overbought territory a mix of calls and stock would give greater profit potential as well as greater downside protection. i.e., 3 calls for 100 shares each against 100 shares held long. Note that only one of these calls is a covered call; the other two are "naked" and require margin. They are also carried in the number 3 a/c.

Play 4   Short stock, buy a protective call [or calls].

Examples of this have already been given (Chapter 7). Ed Thorp's play of buying calls that control more stock than has been sold short falls into this category.

Play 5   Buy a put, hoping to trade stock against it.

The first part of this play is naked. An over-the-counter PUT is bought, which (hopefully) develops profit as the stock declines. When oversold territory is reached, stock is bought. Further decline in the stock is protected by the put. If the stock rises, as planned, it can be traded against the put during the life of the put. This play is only given for completeness. I have no experience at it. (*A similar play would involve selling a naked call with the idea of buying stock to trade against it once a profit had been achieved*).

c] Spreading

Play 6   Write a bearish spread either 1:1, or a multiple bearish spread.

A 1:1 bearish spread when the M.B.I. is in over-bought territory in a bear market is one of the *safest plays on the market*.

Play 7   Spread puts on the CBOE.

If *and when* puts are traded on the CBOE. (This is fully discussed in Chapter 12).

When the market is in *oversold* condition, the same possibilities for trading the long side exist. Namely, (a) skinny-dipping, (b) hedging, and (c) spreading.

LONG SIDE OF THE MARKET

a] **Skinny-dipping**

Play 8   Buy stock, warrants or calls.

Most people just buy stocks and never do anything else. Too frequently they do not protect their naked position by using stops, and all too frequently they do *not* buy in oversold but in *overbought* territory, with, of course, inferior results. Please accept that you are just as much at general market risk in a naked long position as you are in a naked short position, the only difference being that dividends are credited to the long position while they are debited to the short position.

b] **Hedging**

Play 9   Buy stock, sell out-of-the-money option.

As previously discussed, this does not give much downside protection.

Play 10   Buy stock, buy protective put.

At the present time this would have to be a regular over-the-counter put.

Play 11   Buy call hoping to short stock against it.

This is the reverse of Play 5, but the situation never gets off the ground unless the call appreciates first.

c] **Spreading**

Play 12 Set up a bullish spread either 1:1 or a multiple bullish spread or a multiple neutral spread.

We have already examined the possibilities of a multiple neutral spread set up for IBM options. If you have the money to margin such a spread *this is a great way to go.*

Play 14 Set up a bullish spread with puts when the CBOE trades them.

This will be fully discussed in Chapter 12. Note there is no Play 13—I'm not superstitious but maybe you are.

With so many choices, how is a decision reached? Actually, as soon as you get into CBOE trading you will find that certain plays appeal to you and you will tend to concentrate on these plays. *The really important thing is to be on the correct side of the market.* (See Master Game Plan later in this chapter). There is also one other important point. If you have relied heavily on your broker's advice in the past, this is the time to break yourself of that habit, because from now on you will be relying on the Moving Balance System and on yourself. You will know more about the particular situation you have picked out than he does. Have the map in front of you and without a word of explanation give your order to him. Because there are so many different options, make sure he repeats the order back to you. Also, check the confirmation slips when they arrive to make sure they show the correct month and strike price.

As far as the actual mechanics of setting up a hedge are concerned, I think it is better to set up the sell side first and then immediately thereafter the buy side. I have not been too successful trying to "scalp" a little on setting up one side of a position, while waiting to set up the other side. (Note a 1:1 spread can be given to your broker in terms of the basis and the spread can be set up simultaneously). Since the idea is to have protection, not only should both sides be undertaken together, but in most cases they should be terminated together.

But the problems of stock selection, as well as those of option selection, have to be met successfully because one cannot "buy the market" except by buying a mutual fund, and a mutual fund is not really the best short term trading vehicle.

STOCK SELECTION

The Moving Balance Indicator gives an accurate view of the market as a whole but how are suitable stocks for purchase or short sale found? If you are going skinny-dipping, you should try to buy stocks of strong relative strength and sell those of weak relative strength. Relative strength of any stock is determined by dividing the closing price of the stock by the closing price of the New York Comp. (The Dow-Jones Industrial Index closing price may also be used). If the stock acts stronger than the New York Comp., the ratio will increase. (Weekly plotting of Friday's closing ratio is adequate). Obviously, if the ratio decreases the stock is acting more weakly than the New York Comp.

The following table gives the relative strength of McDonalds Corp. (MCD) for the period 3/7/75 to 6/13/75.

Relative strength of MCD (plotted against New York Comp.)

3/7/75	0.98
3/14/75	0.95
3/21/75	0.97
3/27/75	0.99
4/4/75	1.10
4/11/75	1.06
4/18/75	1.07
4/25/75	1.15
5/2/75	1.13
5/9/75	1.13
5/16/75	1.16
5/23/75	1.14
5/30/75	1.11
6/6/75	1.06
6/13/75	1.07

Using this system, MCD was a buy on 4/4/75 (when the M.B.I. was 39 and the stock then 47.2) and a sell on 5/9/75 (M.B.I. 65, stock 54.0).

Gerald Appel's 12 day trading oscillator (Chapter 6) can also be used successfully for individual stocks. Using the oscillator, overbought and oversold areas may be identified when the oscillator readings approach 12-15% of the value of the underlying stock. What I like to do is to add up the daily net gain (loss) on an accumulative basis. The figures for the same period are:

Accumulated 12 day trading oscillator

MCD

3/27/75	− 1.4
4/4/75	+ 7.9
4/11/75	+ 33.3
4/18/75	+ 50.0
4/25/75	+ 64.9
5/2/75	+ 97.1
5//9/75	+ 119.7
5/16/75	+ 141.4
5/23/75	+ 149.9
5/30/75	+ 144.1
6/6/75	+ 122.0
6/13/75	+ 106.1

Here the sell signal is not given until 5/30/75 (M.B.I. 53). The stock closed exactly at 54.0 on that day also.

OPTION SELECTION

In a hedged or spread position, the problems of stock and option selection are made a great deal easier. The option writer is looking for the largest percentage premium; the buyer for the least. Percentage premiums should be annualized for comparison. The formula I use is as follows:

$$\frac{(\text{Present Option Price} + \text{Exercise Price} - \text{Present Price of Stock}) \; 12 \times 100}{\text{Present Price of Stock} \times \text{number of months to expiration}}$$

It is important to realize that the best percentage returns are to be made by out-of-the-money options, *provided the stock advances.* This is an *up market* play, because while the percentage return is the best, the downside protection is the least. A single example should suffice. Stock, STK, is trading at 48.5. The Oct. 50 option is trading at 3.5, the Oct. 45 at 6.5. Let's say the option has four months to run. The Oct. 50 percentage premium is as follows:

$$\frac{3.5 + 50 - 48.5}{48.5} \times \frac{12}{4} \times 100 = 30.9\%$$

i.e., If the stock is called at 50, the writer makes 30.9% (less commissions) annualized. How does the Oct. 45 writer make out? His percentage return is:

$$\frac{6.5 + 45 - 48.5}{48.5} \times \frac{12}{4} \times 100 = 18.6\%$$

Clearly, if the stock is called at 45 he doesn't do as well, but he has 6.5 points of downside protection versus 3.5 points obtained by writing the 50 option.

So when the M.B.I. is in an uptrend, go for out-of-the-money options. And by the opposite line of thought, when the market is in a downtrend, either ratio-write (sell 2 or more options for each 100 shares of stock held) or write in-the-money options that still have a useful premium. This insures (just about) some profit as well as good downside protection.

The stocks with the most percentage premium for their options are volatile stocks paying small dividends—stocks like Avon, Disney, McDonalds, and Polaroid. The usual formula given for assessing volatility is as follows:

$$\text{Volatility} = \frac{\text{high of year} - \text{low of year}}{\frac{1}{2}\,(\text{high of year} + \text{low of year})}$$

But I have found a better way of assessing true volatility, as the above formula tells you only how much a stock has changed and not how many times (which is really what volatility is all about). What I do in evaluating a stock is find the number of times the stock in question *changes 10%* in the course of a year, taking low to high to next low. A stock that rises from 15 to 50, but changes 10% in either direction 5 or 6 times, is clearly more volatile than one that only does so once or twice. And the same is even more important on the downside.

It is time, I believe, to give my Moving Balance System Master Game Plan for all markets.

MASTER GAME PLAN FOR ALL MARKETS USING THE MOVING BALANCE SYSTEM

1) *Identify the trend of the market.*
    Plot the value of the New York Comp. for the day the M.B.I. changes from below 60 to above 60. Also plot the New York Comp. value for the next day that the M.B.I. changes from above 60 to below 60. In effect, one is plotting an M.B.I. value of 60 against the corresponding value of the New York Comp. Continue plotting whenever the M.B.I. crosses the 60 mark.

    In exactly the same way, plot changes involving an M.B.I. value of 40 (Figure 15).

    A) *In a strongly trended up market* as in early 1975.
        There will be more crossings of M.B.I. 60 than M.B.I. 40 (which will lag behing), and the value of the New York Comp. will rise as time progresses (Figure 15).

    B) *In a strongly trended down market* as in mid-1974.
        There will be more crossings of M.B.I. 40 than M.B.I. 60 (which will lag behind), and the value of the New York Comp. will fall.

    C) *In a sideways market* (February - June 1973).
        There will be no M.B.I. 60 crossings, many 40 crossings and a high-low difference between M.B.I. reversals of only about 25 points. (In strongly trended markets, reversals are about 40 M.B.I. points apart).

2) *Hold 200 [or more] shares of any stock.*
    This is because commission costs decrease as the number of options traded increase.

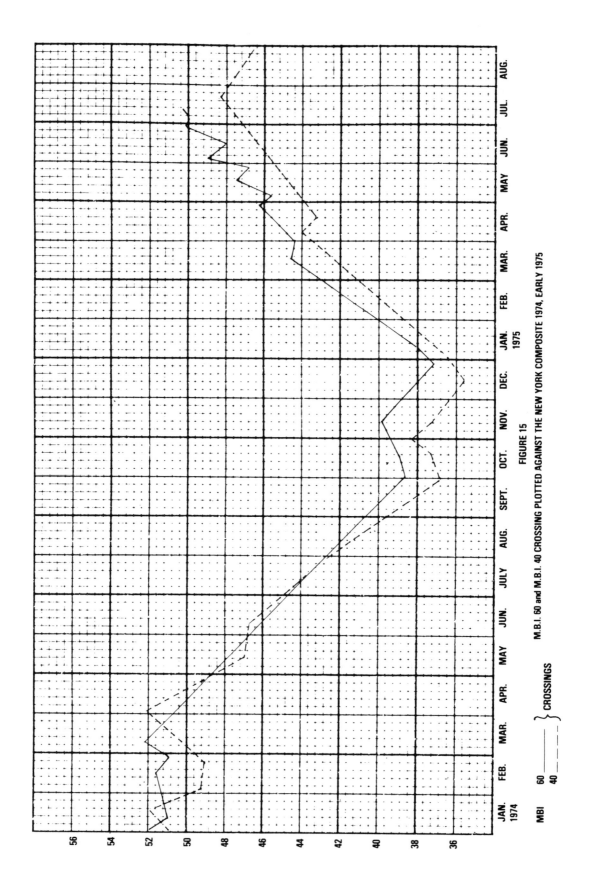

FIGURE 15

M.B.I. 60 and M.B.I. 40 CROSSING PLOTTED AGAINST THE NEW YORK COMPOSITE 1974, EARLY 1975

MBI   60 ————
      40 ———— } CROSSINGS

150

3)   *Regard stock as a prospective "perpetual holding."*
Stock held enables covered writing of calls to be made without posting margin—naked calls must be margined (Chapter 11).

4)   *At M.B.I. big wave high reversals.*
    A)   *Up market high.*
       1)   Stock *higher* than at previous M.B.I. low.
Write slightly in or slightly out-of-the-money covered calls with good percentage premium.
       2)   Stock *lower.*
          a)   Write covered calls deep in-the-money, or
          b)   Set up a multiple neutral spread with higher strike *above* present stock price.

    B)   *Down market high.*
       1)   Stock *higher* than at previous M.B.I. low.
          a)   Write covered calls deep in-the-money, or
          b)   Ratio write a mix of covered and naked calls.
       2)   Stock *lower.*
          a)   Set up bearish spread if market in strong down trend, or
          b)   Sell naked calls.

    C)   *Sideways market high.*
Set up,
       1)   Butterfly spread, or
       2)   Multiple neutral spread.

5)   *At M.B.I. big wave low reversals.*
    A)   *Up market low.*
       1)   Stock *lower* than at previous M.B.I. high.
Terminate call position if profit satisfactory. Hold stock naked until next high.
       2)   Stock *higher.*
          a)   Set up bullish spread if market in strong up trend, or
          b)   Buy calls.

    B)   *Down market low.*

    1)   Stock *lower* that at previous M.B.I. high.

        Terminate call position as above. Write out-of-the-money calls if some protection is required.

    2)   Stock *higher.*

        Do nothing or set up multiple neutral spread.

  C) *Sideways market low.*

        Terminate position only if profit satisfactory.

note: Spreads usually take at least 2 M.B.I. cycles to generate profit *so only set up spreads in consonance with the trend of the market.*

This system will not guarantee profit in the market—nothing will—but it presents a logical way of dealing in the market and with its varying conditions, and if applied as described should produce more successes than failures.

Now it is time to examine the results achieved in 1974 and early 1975.

CHAPTER 10

RESULTS IN 1974 AND 1975

Chapter 10

Results In 1974 And 1975

"Res ipsa loquitur."

This means "the thing speaks for itself" and is an acceptable legal device for assessing evidence. In this Chapter, I want to consider not only some of the results that I achieved but what could be achieved by application of the Moving Balance System to *any* of the stocks on the C.B.O.E. We have to find answers to three questions in order to assess the system:

1) Can the Moving Balance System be shown to work such that the results speak for themselves?

2) Can it further be shown to work without excessively nimble positioning and superior portfolio management?

3) Can a previous loser be shown to come out ahead using the system?

At this point, it is well to realize that all success in the market is relative. No one *ever* buys at the very bottom and sells at the very top, as the scene is always changing and never ends. In the middle of 1973, when Polaroid was changing hands around 140 dollars per share, who would ever have thought that it would fade to 14 1/8 dollars per share a year later. If any financial expert had ever said so, his membership of "the club" would have been forfeit. If he had really felt terribly bearish about the stock, he might have given 60 as an ultimate downside projection, but 14 1/8?!! Come, come, as they say in England.

I think at this point I should admit that many of my friends are REAL financial experts. I live in Beverly, Massachusetts, on the north shore of Boston, with its mutual fund empires. I know well the managers of three of the largest mutual funds. Between them, these men control several billion dollars of other people's money. I also know several trustees and investment counselors. All these men are "pro's." I have given up talking to them about the market, as there is a peculiar glassy look they get when I start using expressions like spread trading, or bearish hedge, or I refer to my indicator. I can't say I blame them. I am sure I would find it distinctly annoying if they started shooting pathological terms at me without having had a proper training in pathology. The only flaw I have found with any of their expertise is that it is "bull-market" expertise. As Gerald Appel, in his new book, *Double Your Money Every Three Years,* remarks, "When you come right down to it, buying mutual funds is, essentially, buying the stock market." Obviously, 1974 was no year to buy the stock market, and my performance was greatly superior in 1974 to any that my friends could have provided for me in their mutual funds or by their advice.

One of the drug houses puts out a "Physician's Financial Letter." It carries a section giving a recommended portfolio, and the latest edition has just arrived. In 1974, 10 recommendations were made. 7 are now down an average of 32%, 1 stock is unchanged, 1 up slightly and 1 up 27%. All are listed as "hold!" Recommendations from 1973, also listed as hold, fared even worse.

Well, in 1974, while the market was declining by about 30%, I reduced my $10,000 lost to the market—the figure I mentioned earlier—by $3,694 actual profit while maintaining at the end of the year 93% of my equity. My previous best year was an actual loss of "only" $748 in 1973 when I was beginning to get the hang of the system that became the Moving Balance System. (But my equity declined 17%).

At this point it must be obvious that I have only a small amount of money in the market. Haven't I got a hell of a nerve writing a book when I cannot show how I doubled at least $100,000? Well, yes I have, but I have given my reasons for writing this book. I know the system is a good one and I am happy to share it with anyone who wants to try it. Far from "wrecking the system" if, by chance, a large number of people should suddenly use it, I think the reverse would be more likely, as the Moving Balance Indicator would show wider and even more clearly defined swings. And just to complete the record for 1974, I had 15 successful against 5 unsuccessful trades for the NET gain mentioned. And I now know quite a bit more than I did at the beginning of 1974, so that in 1975, by the judicious use of spreading, I hope to improve on my 3:1 success ratio. Remember—if the system is a good system it will work without reference to the size of the stake involved. And at this point, if I had $100,000 to invest I know just how I would go about doing it when the M.B.I. told me it was time to move. (I would use Treasury Bills or convertible bonds as margin for the sell side of a multiple spread and use cash for the buy side. A conservative estimate of the likely return counting the interest from the Treasury Bills or bonds—20-30% per annum).

I think the Moving Balance System will give anyone, who is prepared to do a certain amount of work on it and put in a certain amount of thought at it, self-confidence, protection and peace of mind. In 1974, the market had a pretty disastrous down turn in mid-year (Figure 7). We have already seen in the Polaroid situation how judicious hedging could have protected against a loss of 72% in the value of the parent stock. The position was undertaken on 6/7/74 at a Moving Balance Indicator reading of 54—i.e., Zone 4. Clearly, we have to play the short side from this zone and Play 3 was set up in the example given earlier. Actually, Play 6 would have given some interesting profits directly. Remember, in a bearish spread, the parent stock is not purchased.

Play 6   Set up bearish multiple spread.
        Here we have to go back and see what the other PRD options were on 6/7/74.

PRD	Oct. 60	1.4
	Oct. 45	4.4
	Oct. 40	6.8

How about the following play?

SELL

	Debit	Credit
3 Oct. 40 at 6.8		2040
BUY		(6.8 x 3)
2 Oct. 45 at 4.4	880	
	(4.4 x 2)	

The maximum profit is obviously at 40 or below as both options will be worthless = 2040 – 880 = *11.6 points*. The upside breakeven point should be able to be devised from Formula 6, but in this case the equation does not balance (try it) as the breakeven point is *below the higher strike*. The formula to use under this circumstance is Formula 10.

Formula 10 Formula for upside breakeven point for multiple bearish spread when "B" is below higher strike.

$$\text{Total AR} - (B - LS) \text{ number calls written} = \text{total AP}$$

i.e.,   6.8 x 3 = Total amount received

= 20.4

4.4 x 2 = Total amount paid
= 8.8

$$20.4 - (B - 40)\ 3 = 8.8$$

$$20.4 - (3B - 120) = 8.8$$

$$20.4 - 8.8 = 3B - 120$$

$$11.6 + 120 = 3B$$

$$131.6 = 3B$$

$$B = \frac{131.6}{3}$$

$$= 43.9 \quad [43.86]$$

At *43.9* therefore, the Sell Side will show the following profit:

SELL SIDE

	Debit	Credit
Each 40 option worth 3.9	1170	2040
	(3.9 x 3)	(6.8 x 3)
Profit = <u>8.7 points</u>		

and the Buy Side the following loss:

BUY SIDE

	Debit	Credit
Each 45 option is worthless	880	0
	(4.4 x 2)	

Loss = <u>8.8 points</u>

As we saw, the stock fell drastically and the total profit of $1160 would have been made. This would have been pure profit, as the parent stock on which the spread is based would not have been purchased. Notice that a 1:1 bearish spread, i.e.,

SELL

	Debit	Credit
1 Oct. 40		680
BUY		
1 Oct. 45	440	

could only yield a profit of "the basis"—the difference in option price received and price paid = 2.2 points. This would not be a satisfactory situation as the possible loss would be greater. Possible loss is given by strike spread less basis = 5.0 – 2.2 = 2.8 points.

What about the other bearish plays? Well, since the stock got the you-know-what-kicked out of it, any of these plays would have been profitable.

Polaroid did indeed do very poorly compared to many of the other stocks on the Big Board. How much of the success I claim for the system is really attributable to the poor performance of a stock like Polaroid?

Well, I have the answer to that one. In Figure 7 the M.B.I. was plotted for 1974. Obviously, there are big wave reversal points on the following occasions. (M.B.I. readings in parenthesis).

HIGH	**LOW**	
Jan. 4 (64)	Feb. 13 (28)	
Mar. 5 (64)	Apr. 9 (21)	Average High 61.2
June 7 (54)	July 10 (17)	Average Low 20.8
July 24 (55)	Oct. 4 (16)	<u>Difference 40.4</u>
Oct. 18 (69)	Nov. 21 (22)	
(Average 61.2)	(Average 20.8)	

What were the C.B.O.E. stocks doing during this time? The following table (VIII) tells the story.

TABLE VIII

ANALYSIS OF C.B.O.E. STOCKS AT BIG WAVE REVERSAL

	HI 1/4	LO 2/13	HI 3/5	LO 4/9	HI 6/7	LO 7/10	HI 7/24	LO 10/4	HI 10/18	LO 11/21
ATT	51.4	51.7	52.6	48.5	48.0	43.5	44.2	40.7	45.5	43.6
ARC	111.2	96.5	101.7	91.2	93.0	86.4	89.5	76.5	88.7	88.7
AVP	57.2	47.5	55.2	52.2	51.2	36.5	33.2	20.0	24.4	28.5
BS	34.0	31.8	34.7	32.8	30.2	31.0	32.5	24.6	27.2	26.7
BC	15.2	15.5	17.7	16.0	15.2	10.5	12.8	7.6	8.5	9.8
EK	111.2	100.2	107.8	107.8	114.2	98.4	95.0	60.7	69.8	67.8
XON	97.8	82.5	86.8	80.4	77.7	70.2	77.0	55.7	67.2	59.5
F	40.6	44.5	50.6	49.1	53.2	47.8	48.5	35.7	35.4	31.0
GW	25.5	24.0	26.2	26.2	24.6	19.5	20.4	18.6	20.6	22.8
GWF	19.2	21.5	21.2	18.5	19.7	10.5	12.5	11.6	13.2	13.7
IBM	230.8	233.5	240.5	233.5	229.2	215.0	221.0	156.2	184.2	170.5
INA	37.0	35.8	37.4	33.7	28.8	24.8	24.0	22.2	25.4	26.6
ITT	29.2	26.4	25.5	21.8	21.8	19.4	20.1	14.7	16.0	15.5
HR	27.4	25.0	29.2	26.7	27.0	23.0	23.5	19.6	19.8	20.2
KMG	89.6	75.0	79.0	70.7	72.5	61.5	64.0	51.6	66.0	67.5
KS	32.2	33.5	37.0	30.2	38.4	32.1	30.0	19.5	25.2	23.5
LTR	22.8	19.2	22.4	19.7	17.2	14.8	16.1	11.6	13.0	14.7
MMM	78.0	70.0	76.2	74.7	76.2	72.2	70.0	48.6	58.2	53.0
MCD	53.0	49.7	57.2	52.6	59.0	42.4	44.0	21.2	32.2	32.7
MRK	77.2	73.5	81.0	80.7	83.7	77.1	73.5	51.0	59.2	64.5
MTC	55.8	54.7	59.6	59.0	68.7	61.4	64.0	45.2	51.4	42.5
NWA	20.0	22.4	25.0	22.8	26.0	20.5	21.8	13.6	16.2	14.5
PZL	28.4	25.4	26.0	26.2	20.2	15.8	20.0	13.5	16.6	17.5
PRD	66.5	71.0	83.2	60.5	41.7	31.0	29.1	15.8	19.7	20.2
RCA	20.4	18.5	20.8	18.6	16.7	14.5	13.6	10.6	11.0	10.8
S	84.0	83.5	87.7	82.5	89.8	77.7	77.2	45.2	50.2	45.8
SY	43.2	38.6	42.5	39.7	42.4	36.1	37.5	24.2	28.2	26.7
TXN	101.6	96.0	107.2	95.7	98.8	89.2	85.4	60.2	62.6	74.5
UPJ	64.7	56.2	71.5	67.6	86.2	77.2	76.2	45.5	41.8	46.0
WY	41.2	36.0	39.6	41.0	39.4	36.4	37.0	25.2	31.2	27.4
XRX	114.5	107.0	118.7	113.6	124.8	107.2	109.1	60.7	68.5	56.2

These figures were taken from Barron's, which only gives the C.B.O.E. stocks and options on a weekly basis, so there will be minor differences between the figures given here and the actual closing price of any particular stock on the day of a big wave reversal if that day did not happen to be a Friday. But the differences will be minor, and the table shows what it is designed to show—namely the way that the C.B.O.E. stocks move in unison with the M.B.I. Indeed, a trader could have done quite well just buying and selling most of the stocks at big wave reversal points. For instance, consider the sequence of EXXON (XON).

Let us imagine trades were made at each big wave reversal point as follows:

At initial big wave high - sell short.
At next big wave low (a) cover short.
                       (b) buy.
At next big wave high (a) sell.
                       (b) sell short.

And so on until the big wave low on Nov. 21. The sequence for Exxon (XON) would be:

		Profit
1.14	sell short at 97.8	
2.14	(a) cover short at 82.5	15.3 (97.8 – 82.5)
	(b) buy at 82.5	
3.5	(a) sell at 86.8	4.3 (86.8 – 82.5)
	(b) sell short at 86.8	

etc., etc.

The total profit (less a considerable amount of commission I regret) would have been *78.1 points* and this would have been achieved by using the Moving Balance System in this way *without regard to any indicator* other than the M.B.I. Some stocks did better than others, of course. RCA only gained 9.4 points, whereas I.B.M. gained 133.7 points. But this demonstrates to my satisfaction that, by and large, these stocks fluctuate in tune with the M.B.I. and that using the M.B.I. alone, a considerable amount of money could have been made. The system indeed "speaks for itself."

But to take a naked position is risky, and hedging or spreading would have been preferable. Were there any good plays on the buy side during 1974? In the last chapter, you may have noticed that I gave more "sell" choices than buy choices. There is a reason for this, because the C.B.O.E. does not yet trade PUTS. Also, consider for a moment the situation when the market is heavily overbought. It is possible to write naked options which carry a good premium and collect the premium when the stock tumbles. However, on the buy side you have to *pay* a premium which you lose as the option matures *whether the stock goes up or down*. If the stock goes up, the option appreciates also and the loss of the premium is not significant. But if the stock declines, then all is lost.

Actually, as soon as I began to understand what I was doing I developed a *preference for the short side of the market.* On the short side, you *receive* the premium when you write a call and you keep it whether the stock goes up or down.

But there were some good plays to be made on the buy side. I made out quite well on buying options on Pennzoil and Polaroid during the year. The idea is to buy an option only at a low M.B.I. reading and sell it when the M.B.I. gets up into the high country. The important thing to realize is that option buying, as a naked play, is very risky in an overall bear market as the entire option price may well be lost (it is estimated that around 60% of calls bought expire unexercised, the buyers of these calls losing the total amount of money required to take the position). Remember, preservation of capital is essential and you cannot make money losing money.

Using the retrospectroscope, however, how would the purchaser of options have made out from the tables? Remember that an option is a *wasting asset*. Let's examine a position taken at a big wave low, say in I.B.M. There was a big wave low on Feb. 13th. The I.B.M. options then were listed as follows:

				IBM
Feb. 13	Apr.	270	1.4	234
	Apr.	240	7.8	
	July	270	4.7	
	July	240	14.2	
	Oct.	270	8	
	Oct.	240	18	

The stock was trading at 234. Well, at the next big wave high (March 5th) the stock was trading at 240 and the options traded as follows:

				Gain in points
Mar. 5	Apr.	270	1.6	0.2
	Apr.	240	11.5	3.7
	July	270	5.7	1.0
	July	240	19.5	5.3
	Oct.	270	10.2	2.2
	Oct.	240	25.0	7.0

Obviously, the stock has appreciated 6 points and the options have appreciated by the figure in the far right-hand column. The purchaser of the Oct 240 option would have done much better (on a percentage basis) than the holder of the common stock. But, March 5th had a high reading on the M.B.I. of 64. Under these circumstances, on a Moving Balance System basis, the sensible thing to do would be to close out the position (with a profit) as M.B.I. readings over 60 are not maintained for any length of time. The only time you can hang on is during the earliest stages after setting up a position in Zones 4 or 5. Just to underline the point, *all* the I.B.M. options just discussed expired *worthless*.

In any down year, there will be sharp rallies—call them what you will. And some good profits can be made on the buy side if any money happens to be around to put into such a situation. For instance, on Oct. 11th the market closed up 73.61 points on the Dow, the M.B.I. having risen from a low of 16 on Oct. 4th to 54 on the 11th. It made it to 69 on the 18th, but let us just consider that one week. In the 20 most active stocks list, we find several C.B.O.E. stocks. McDonald's catches our eye, having advanced 7.2 points to 28.6. What did the options do and how would Play 9 have fared if undertaken at the beginning of the week? There were several MCD options outstanding. The April *25* went up 3.8 points, the most of any of them. Let's imagine that on 10/4/74 100 shares of MCD were bought for 21.4. The only option listed with any real value is the April *25* going for 2.8. Suppose 100 shares of MCD were bought and simultaneously the out-of-the-money Apr. 25 option was sold. What would have happened? When MCD was at 21.4 the call sold effectively reduces the price to 21.4 − 2.8 = 18.6. But it is not callable until the stock reaches at least 25, so the profit is 25 − 18.6 = 6.4 points. Actually, the outright purchase of common stock would have been more profitable. But why not wait until the stock rises, say to the 28.6

it did make in a week, and then write an out-of-the-money option on it, say the Apr *30* and receive an additional x points? Well, that's fine if the stock rises, but offers no protection when the stock is bought.

Actually, when the parent stock moves up or down so will the options ride with it. You can see the tremendous possibilities for all the different plays I have mentioned when you realize the number of options of differing strikes and expiration dates traded against each CBOE stock, and with the American Exchange becoming more active, both option buyers and option sellers will have increasing future opportunities. One of my favorite plays is the multiple spread play (12) given in detail in the chapter on spreading. Depending on the expectation one has for a stock's decline, the downside can be engineered to break-even, lose a little, or gain a little, depending on how high the stock is expected to go. Remember, the maximum gain is always exactly at the higher strike price.

The table of the behavior of the CBOE stocks reveals three very interesting facts: 1) If the price of an individual stock at a big wave high reversal fails to make it above its previous big wave low reversal value, it is bearish for the individual stock. Merck is a good example.

	Big-wave low value	77.1	(7/10/74)
next	Big-wave high value	73.5	(7/24/74)
next	Big-wave low value	51.0	

2) When the situation as in no. 1 applies to several CBOE stocks (as it did on 6/7/74) hang on to your hat, batten down the hatches and prepare to be a real bear.

3) When several stocks at a big low close higher than their previous value at a big wave high (as they did on 11/21/74) a market reversal on the upside is due. The M.B.I. stayed low while the market itself bottomed out in early December 1974, but then the M.B.I. advanced strongly in early 1975 to record high figures.

1974 was not a good year by any standards for most people in the market. I have claimed success for the Moving Balance Indicator in predicting market activity in 1974. But would it be of any use in a year of strong bullish activity? I do not yet have the data for the whole of 1975 which started off so bullishly, but I do have the data for a strong upmove that started on Aug. 22, 1973 and carried the Dow from 845.5 on Aug. 22nd to 991.8 on Oct. 12th. The low and high M.B.I. readings were 24 and 80 respectively—the low and high M.B.I. points in 1974 were 16 and 69—a difference in 8 points on the low figure and 11 on the high figure. Remember, the M.B.I. has been multiplied by 2, so I think these two sets of figures are comparable. I would expect higher M.B.I. readings in a bullish market, anyway, because of the effect of the 10 day Advancing Volume. The point is that the M.B.I. high of 80, which occurred on Sept. 27th, was not maintained and down it fell, and not long after the Dow fell. The crucial readings are given in Table IX.

TABLE IX: M. B. I. READINGS–DOW

Date	M.B.I. Reading	Dow
8/22/73	24	845.5 (Intra-day low)
9/27/73	80	964.6 (Intra-day high)
10/12/73	65	991.8 (Intra-day high)
12/3/73	28	789.3 (Intra-day low)

The final figures are not in yet for the markedly bullish activity that occurred early in 1975. On Jan. 13, 1975 the M.B.I. hit 76 and I decided to enter a 1:1 bearish spread in Great Western Financial, and also to write a naked call on Avon, realizing, if the Avon position went against me, that any loss would be ordinary income loss. I have said that I do not advise a naked play, but I had already accumulated some ordinary income gains in 1975 (from covering some Jan 75 options), so I could put any loss on the Avon position against these gains.

At any rate, the M.B.I. fell to 49 *without any real weakness* in the underlying market, so I covered the Avon call for a 3 point profit. The Sell Side of the Great Western situation was called on me for a small loss. (Note I have been called as much as two and a half month's prior to the expiration date of a call. This gives a rather insecure feeling and is the only disadvantage to spread trading. It also explains the attractiveness of other plays, particularly shorting stocks against calls long. That position is safe until the expiration of the call). So the M.B.I. corrected from 76 to 49 without any real change in the market, and shortly thereafter both the market and the M.B.I. took off. The M.B.I. made my all time high on Feb. 5, 1975 with a reading of 85. This indicates great imbalance and great buying pressure. When demand like this builds up, it is not easy to discourage it. Readings of 80 and over should *not provoke immediate bearish action* because they denote *very strong demand*. It is imperative to watch the relationship of the M.B.I. and market once a very high M.B.I. reading has been made. Disparity between the M.B.I. and the market means one of two things (under these conditions):

1) The market will reverse and this move should begin within 12 trading days.

2) The market is going higher and the M.B.I. will reverse.

We have seen how very high M.B.I. readings (80 and over) top out about 11 or 12 days before the market. An interval of this length is only seen when very strong demand is present. In a bear market high, M.B.I. reversals call the tops very closely and, even in a bull market, M.B.I. reversals in the 70's do not precede a market turndown by more than 0-5 days.

However, when terrific buying pressure comes in there are two useful rules to remember and one formula to apply. The first rule is the *12 day rule*, which states that the market will correct within 12 trading days of an M.B.I. high reversal. I derived this 12 day rule empirically, but it seems to work. Here's what to do. Pay particular attention to the relationship between the Dow and the M.B.I. as the 12th trading day after an unusually high M.B.I. reading approaches. For the rally in question, on the 11th trading day after the high of 85 on February 5, 1975, the market closed at 749.7 with an intra-day high of 757.4 (February 21, 1975). The M.B.I. was 63 and the New York Comp. had risen $1.75 ($43.70 - $41.95). I took all this to mean that the market, while still definitely over-bought, was going to go higher, as continued strong demand was present. Indeed, there is a backup to the 12 day rule just mentioned, and it is the second rule, the *$1.50 rule*. This rule states that if the New York Comp. rises by $1.50 or more within 12 days of an M.B.I. high, serious imbalance is present, and with it the strong possibility of a continuation of the up-move.

The formula to apply is this:

Projected next reversal of N.Y. Comp.

= value of N.Y. Comp. at M.B.I. high reversal less value of N.Y. Comp. at previous M.B.I. low reversal x 0.4 + value of N.Y. Comp. at M.B.I. high reversal.

For the rally in question

value of N.Y. Comp. at M.B.I. high = 41.95
value of N.Y. Comp. at previous M.B.I. low = 37.71

Projected reversal = (41.95 – 37.71) 0.4 + 41.95
                   = 1.70 + 41.95
                   = 43.65

Actual reversal   = 43.70

This formula does not always work out so well, of course, but I have not yet found more than a 40% overshoot (0.4) in the value of the New York Comp. when the M.B.I. corrects.

The New York Comp. corrected from 43.70 to 42.09 before turning back up. Remember, we are dealing with daily figures and a short-term indicator.

I would like to emphasize that it is only when the market gets seriously imbalanced that one has to fine tune the M.B.I. to the New York Comp. and the market so carefully. In less turbulent times, the M.B.I. will call the tops well on its own. But when a group of circumstances come together to fuel the market, strange things happen. The only force I know that really has a *predictable* effect on the market is the availability of money and its cost as determined by the Federal Reserve. When money is easy, so is the living on Wall Street. In early March 1975, we had the following circumstances: (1) The Fed was priming the pump. (2) Institutions had money to invest in stocks. (3) Money was being transferred from the money-market high-interest funds (since the interest rates had fallen) back into the stock market. (4) Investor psychology was bullish, as no one wanted to ''miss the boat.''

I was bearish over the near-term because of the unbalanced buying, but I felt reasonably bullish for 1975. What plays might have been appropriate at the time? The following should have been considered:

1) A calendar spread.
2) A butterfly or multiple neutral spread.
2) A bearish spread *with wide basis.*
4) The Burroughs situation (Chapter 8).

Please note: This was not the time to be an out and out bear.

The market, of course, does do what it has to do, regardless of what I, or anyone else, thinks it ought to do. All I really knew was that the strongly overbought position would at some point be corrected, as such imbalance *cannot* be sustained indefinitely. And that somewhere in time the market would become deeply oversold again with gloom and doom around our ears.

My results, then, in 1974 were fine. They were much better using my system than I had ever managed to do before, and I had tried, as I said, other systems. The great thing, I think, is to become thoroughly familiar with a system—to develop a feel for it. The Moving Balance System is built on an indicator that, for the most part, moves with the market. However, I hope I have shown how use can be made of the disparity that may occur from time to time between this indicator and the market.

Now we have to consider some practical aspects of stock and option trading, which we can pull together under the general title—Portfolio Management.

CHAPTER 11

PORTFOLIO MANAGEMENT

Portfolio Management

There are several aspects to be considered:

1) *Equipment*

The following are essential.
a) *A notebook.*
   Either a notebook such as No. 31-386, The National Blank Book, Holyoke, Massachusetts 01040 (you will have to rule the columns), or some already columned paper (National 42-383) is necessary for tabulating the data and for calculating the M.B.I. The New York Stock Exchange Composite Index (N.Y. Comp.) is also recorded as a quick reference point to the state of the market. Table X gives a typical page recording over a month's market activity.

b) *A calculator; or a combination of adding machine and slide rule.*
   With the reduction in price of pocket calculators, coupled with their portability, the combination of adding machine and slide rule is really obsolete. (The slide rule is for working out the A/D Index). Any small pocket calculator will do. I have a Sharp, model EL-8002, which costs only $30 and is most satisfactory.

c) *Graph paper.*
   For plotting the M.B.I. on a Monday - Wednesday - Friday basis. Keuffel and Esser Co., No. 46-0780 is fine.

TABLE X
DATA FOR CALCULATING THE MBI

1974	MBI	N.Y. Comp	Adv.	Decl.	10 day Adv.	10 day Decl.	A/D	Adv. Vol.	10 day Adv. Vol.	MKDS	10 day MKDS	Assigned MKDS
Sept. 30	31	33.45	257	1162	696.3	707.3	0.98	2570	5380	1.49	1.558	0.5
Oct. 1	27	33.40	598	428	639.1	719.6	0.89	6290	5038	1.96	1.656	-1.0
2		33.44	828	511	658.1	701.4	0.93	5500	5113	1.47	1.710	
3		32.89	403	957	569.9	774.2	0.73	1850	3963	2.22	1.854	-2.5
4	16 △	32.90	688	670	544.1	789.6	0.69	6340	3795	1.21	1.831	
7	22	34.19	1301	228	600.4	745.7	0.80	12590	4618	0.67	1.750	-1.5
8		34.16	875	547	650.4	700.0	0.93	6370	5114	1.79	1.735	
9	33	35.69	1220	264	689.5	670.4	1.03	15520	5950	0.57	1.616	0
10		36.77	1338	261	787.6	599.8	1.31	19470	7773	1.23	1.541	
11	54	37.49	1063	422	857.1	545.0	1.57	13290	8979	0.96	1.356	2.5
14	67	38.36	1199	338	951.3	462.6	2.03	15180	10240	0.74	1.281	3.0
15		37.67	440	1048	935.5	524.6	1.82	3000	9911	1.63	1.249	
16	58	37.12	461	954	898.8	568.9	1.58	3050	9666	1.60	1.262	3.5
17		37.52	765	590	935.0	532.2	1.75	7980	10279	0.78	1.118	
18	69 ▶	38.08	947	468	960.9	512.0	1.88	9690	10614	1.03	1.100	5.0
21	65	38.72	848	528	915.6	542.0	1.70	9300	10285	0.59	1.092	5.0
22		38.57	721	674	900.2	554.7	1.62	7340	10382	1.35	1.048	
23	51	37.54	280	1139	806.2	642.2	1.26	1320	8962	2.15	1.206	4.0
24		37.10	294	1151	701.8	731.2	0.96	3400	7355	0.74	1.157	
25	40 △	37.07	666	640	662.1	753.0	0.88	5800	6606	0.86	1.147	4.5
28	35 △	37.04	521	783	594.3	797.5	0.75	4290	5517	0.71	1.144	4.5
29		38.37	1030	351	653.2	727.8	0.90	11950	6412	0.58	1.039	
30	49	39.12	953	448	702.5	677.2	1.04	14190	7526	0.62	0.941	6.5
31		38.97	699	785	695.9	696.7	1.00	8140	7542	0.88	0.951	
Nov. 1	46	38.94	702	664	671.4	716.3	0.94	5730	7146	1.10	0.958	6.5
4	41	38.53	485	884	635.1	751.9	0.84	3330	6549	1.27	1.026	5.5
5		39.54	991	394	662.1	723.9	0.92	12590	7074	0.38	0.929	
6	53	39.46	882	547	722.3	664.7	1.09	11380	8080	1.44	0.858	7.5
7		39.74	850	543	777.9	603.9	1.29	10640	8804	0.63	0.847	
8	58	39.63	746	596	785.9	599.5	1.31	6860	8910	1.20	0.881	7.0

172

d) *A good daily paper giving the following financial data.*
   1) No. of advancing stocks (on the New York Stock Exchange).
   2) No. of declining stocks (on the New York Stock Exchange).
   3) Advancing volume (on the New York Stock Exchange).
   4) Declining volume (on the New York Stock Exchange).
   5) Closing price of the New York Stock Exchange Index.

Nice to have but not strictly essential are:

e) *The Wall Street Journal*
   The daily charts on the last page are worth the price of the subscription.

f) *Barron's*
   The weekly wizard.

g) *A subscription to an advisory service.*
   To give you a feel for what other people are thinking. Many good ones are available.

h) *Chartcraft point and figure charts for the C.B.O.E. stocks, published by Chartcraft, Inc., Larchmont, N.Y. 10538*
   These are helpful in stock selection at particular M.B.I. periods.

2) *Margin Requirements*

You will need to open a Margin account if you do not already have one. At least $2000 is required initially. Margin accounts come into being as a form of leverage; the idea being to borrow money (at a steep price) from your broker in order to increase the return percentage. Let us consider two transactions—one on a cash basis—the other margined at 50%—i.e., 50% of the money necessary for initiating the position has been borrowed from your friendly broker.

CASH TRANSACTION

	Debit	Credit
Buy CBA stock at 20, sell at 30 100 shares CBA	2000	3000

Profit (less commissions) = 10 points.
This is 10 points on 20 points = 50%.

MARGIN TRANSACTION (50% margin)

	Debit	Credit
100 shares CBA: put up	1000	3000
borrow 1000		

When the position is liquidated the $1000 will be returned to the lender; the amount received will be $2000, $1000 being profit.

This is a profit of 10 points on 10 points of your own money = 100%. What you have borrowed is called the "Debit Balance," and you will pay one point over the prime rate for this money. Your money is the *equity* of the account and the percentage that your money forms of the total market value of the account is the *margin*. Your equity will, of course, vary with the market value of the securities you own. *Initial* margin is the original amount of money you have to put up. The requirements are set by the Federal Reserve and are currently 50%. They have been as high as 90% (in 1959) and may occasionally go—in special situations—to 100%. 100% margin = a cash transaction in which you cannot borrow any money to initiate the position.

In the situation just considered, the stock appreciated, thereby generating *excess equity*. This is carried on the books as a *Special Miscellaneous Account* or SMA. In the CBA situation the stock appreciated from $2000 to $3000. At $3000 the equity (your money) is $3000 less the debit balance (which is $1000) = $2000. However, at $3000 a debit balance of $1500 could be supported (at a 50% margin requirement). This would leave equity at $1500. However, we have just seen that actually equity of $2000 exists. There is obviously $2000 – $1500 = $500 = *excess equity* and this is the SMA. At 50% margin it will have *buying power* of $500 x 100 ÷ 50 = $1000. $1000 worth of securities can be bought (or sold short) without posting additional margin.

The SMA figure is calculated once a week. Notice that if you want to *withdraw* money from a margin account following a closing transaction, only 30% of the total amount involved plus any SMA can be withdrawn. Therefore, do not use your margin account as a temporary haven for funds.

But what if the stock does not appreciate? What indeed. Stock CBA is, in fact, a real dog and starts falling immediately after the position was taken. At 16 the position is as follows:

```
100 shares CBA at 16—value 1600
Debit balance              1000
Equity                      600
```

Equity as % price of stock 600 x 100 ÷ 1600 = 37.5%. This is the *maintenance margin.* The player owns 37.5% of the total market value of the account. The New York Stock Exchange demands maintenance margin of 30%, so if the stock falls further, say to 14, a *margin call* for money to reduce the debit balance will be sent out, as at 14 the equity will be 4 points and 29% of the total market value of the account. If the money is not forthcoming, the broker will sell the stock. Notice that the stock has depreciated 6 on 20 points = 30%—i.e., a margin call is due any time a 30% depreciation in the total market value of the account has occurred.

When the margin in the account is below 50% but above 30% (or 35% depending on the house), the account is *restricted.* Only the following transactions are permitted:

a) Opening transactions at full initial margin for the individual transaction. (you do *not* have to restore the whole account to initial margin requirements).

b) Same day substitutions—dollar for dollar—i.e., securities worth $1000 can be sold and others worth $1000 bought on the same trading day without posting additional margin.

c) Transactions based on the SMA. An account can be restricted but have SMA, as money generated by price appreciation and transferred to the SMA account is left there.

The margin requirements for C.B.O.E. options are as follows:

Purchase requires cash—cannot be margined.
Sale   a) covered options require no additional margin.
         b) naked options have complicated margin requirements.

The following are the New York Stock Exchange requirments; but many brokerage houses make greater demands on their clients.

30% of the market value of the stock plus or minus the difference between stock price and strike price of the option (*plus* if the strike price of option is *below* the present stock price, *minus* if above) less option price received.

There is a minimum margin requirement of $250 per option.

On December 12, 1974 the regulations for true 1:1 spreads were amended. The language is complicated but what it comes down to is this. In a 1:1 spread *the margin required is the maximum possible loss*. So in a 1:1 bullish spread, the margin is the basis (difference in option prices) and in a 1:1 bearish spread it is the strike spread less the basis.

I mentioned earlier that low-priced warrants have unfavorable margin requirements and, though I do not recommend warrant hedging, it is just as well to know that any security valued at $2.50 or below requires $2.50 initial margin. If you want to short a warrant at $1.50, it will cost you $2.50 in collateral!

3) *The Mystique of Short Selling*

If an investor buys a stock for $20 per share and the stock rises to $50 per share and he sells it, the transaction is shown in his account as follows:

	Debit	Credit
100 shares CBA	2000	5000
	(less commissions)	

His profit is obviously 30 points. This may be pounding the nail with the hammer, but he does not make any money unless the stock appreciates in value.

If the stock depreciates and he closes out the position the investor has a loss (no kidding) i.e., the stock falls to 10 = 10 points loss.

	Debit	Credit
100 shares CBA	2000	1000

An investor who buys stock in a company is betting that the stock will appreciate. (That is unless he *plans* for some unknown reason to lose money as the stock drops in value. Many investors *end up* losing money but none really have losing as part of their *conscious* game plan). So, when an investor takes a position in a stock, he is betting that in the future there will be more buyers than sellers of the stock. (He may give you all sorts of good fundamental reasons for his choice and he may describe it in all sorts of fancy terms, but it is a *bet* pure and simple). If there are more buyers than sellers the stock *will* appreciate as the demand for it will be strong. But there has to be a reason for this demand and there are always sellers on the sidelines waiting to knock the price of the stock down—"The stock fell of its own weight." Whereas it can *fall* of its own weight, it never *rises* by its own weight. Which means that the *sellers* actually pack somewhat more punch than the buyers.

But wouldn't it be nice if a profit could be made in reverse—i.e., looking back at the original statement concerning CBA.

	Debit	Credit
100 shares CBA	2000	5000

In the original example the process went from left to right. But since no transaction dates were given, what if the transaction went from right to left—i.e., 5000 were credited and 2000 debited *later*. Obviously, if 5000 were credited that would be the *sale* price and if 2000 were debited that would be the purchase price.

But how on earth can one sell something *one does not own*, because *in order to make a profit*, this is what one would have to do. Then, when the stock declines, it would be bought and the profit shown would be achieved.

This is what short-selling is all about—it is also called going short, being short, or just *short*. The following steps are involved:

a) Securities from another investor's margin account are borrowed. The "lending" investor usually does not know if the securities he owns have been borrowed, as margin account transactions are kept in street-name—the name of the brokerage house. If it is a large house it is usually possible to borrow securities from another investor doing business within the house, i.e., the securities will be in the "cage," the room where they are held. If no securities are available within the house for borrowing, your broker will have to go outside to another house for them. (note: Never try to sell anything short unless your broker has located certificates to borrow—i.e., don't sell short on the expectation that your broker will be *able* to find them. He may *not* be able to in which case you cannot hold a short position). The margin you have to post is collateral to protect the lender.

b)   The short seller now *sells* these securities against 50% of their value as *collateral*. The transaction is carried in his No. 3 account, the short account. The initial margin (50%) that he has to post is *credited* to his regular margin account (the No. 2 account). Notice he does *not* have to pay his broker the usual point over prime carrying charges as he has not borrowed any money. Indeed, the margin posted reduces his debit balance. The *equity* of the short account is always *kept at zero.* This means that if the investor decides to cover the position at any time, he reduces the short account to zero—i.e., the money he is debited for covering = money credited from the short sale. Any profit (or loss) on the position will be reflected in the No. 2 account, because the short account is *marked to the market* each week. It is this mark to the market that adjusts the equity to zero. Any decline in the underlying stock (= profit) will mean money *from* the short account will be transferred *to* the credit of the margin account. The process sounds more complicated than it actually is. What it really is, is a bookkeeping device so that the brokerage house can keep track of the short positions held by their clients. But it certainly makes one's monthly statement look complicated. The trick here is to make sure that the figures to and from the No. 2 and No. 3 accounts correspond; i.e., a debit to the No. 2 account is shown as a credit to the No. 3 account; and vice versa.

If the stock held short *appreciates*, money is transferred *from* the margin account *to* the short account, decreasing the equity in the No. 2 account. It will also increase the debit balance. The debit balance, in other words, *is* affected fluctuations in the No. 3 account because of the mark to the market. But *if no securities are held short,* the debit balance in the No. 2 account will *not* vary with the value of the underlying stock. Unless, of course, the maintenance margin falls and a margin call is sent out to reduce the debit balance.

c) When the investor desires to terminate the position, he buys the stock he has sold short. He "covers" his position (with profit or loss) and the certificates borrowed are returned to the lender.

Short selling is said to be all kinds of terrible things, not the least of which is un-American—"Never sell America short." Its bad reputation goes back to the days of the robber barons and to the heyday of stock manipulation when it was possible to "get a corner" on the market; that is, for a person or group to gain possession of most or all of the certificates of a particular security that have been sold short and to force the short sellers to pay outrageous prices to cover their position. This is called a *short-squeeze*. The opposite to a short-squeeze is to be *bought-in*, when the lender demands return of his securities. I have never been caught in a short-squeeze and do not honestly think that such a possibility is a real danger any more. But I was bought-in once which was a nuisance. I had a profit in the position, but it was a warrant hedge and left the long side unprotected.

It is important to accept that success using the Moving Balance System depends, to a large extent, on playing the short side of the market. It does not feel very dangerous to write a covered option. Indeed, it is very safe. Also, it does not feel like short selling—particularly as the transaction is carried in the No. 2 account, but a form of short selling it is. You are, in effect, selling the true premium short and if you write a naked option the transaction will be carried in the No. 3 account, so there's no doubt about which side of the market you are on in that situation.

There is one other aspect of short selling stock or warrants—the *up-tick rule*. This rule does *not* apply to writing options. In effect, it means that there must have been recently a lower price than the one at which you wish to short the security. The rule is designed to prevent shorting a stock that is falling directly out of bed onto the floor.

Actually, this will not usually be a problem if you decide to use one of the M.B.S. plays described in which stock (or warrants) have to be sold short, because you will only be doing this from Zones 4 or 5, so the stock should be topping out and easy to short.

4) *Initiating the position*

I have already stated that it is wise to initiate both sides of a hedge together. Since only a spread can be executed exactly at the same time, I believe it is better to execute the short or sell side of a hedge transaction before taking the long position. Some brokers are better than others at getting good executions. Also, you will need a broker who has a feel for options and you will need a brokerage house that deals in CBOE and Amex options.

The rules for initiating the position are simple.

a) Wait until the M.B.I. gives readings that at least reach the Zone 4/5 boundary zone for short positions and the 1/2 boundary zone for long positions.

In a *bear* market the zones are as follows:

Zone 5	60 and above
4	49 - 60
3	30 - 49
2	21 - 30
1	21 and below

However, in a *bull* market as shown by the M.B.I. chart for the first six months of 1975, the zones are all higher (Figure 16).

In a *bull* market the zones are as follows:

Zone 5	75 and above
4	64 - 75
3	45 - 64
2	36 - 45
1	36 and below

Important

If an M.B.I. reading above 70 is obtained in what has been a bear market, suspect an underlying change in market direction, and if an M.B.I. reading below 30 is obtained in what has been a bull market, suspect that all may not be well with el toro. Be very cautious at these times.

b) Make a map.

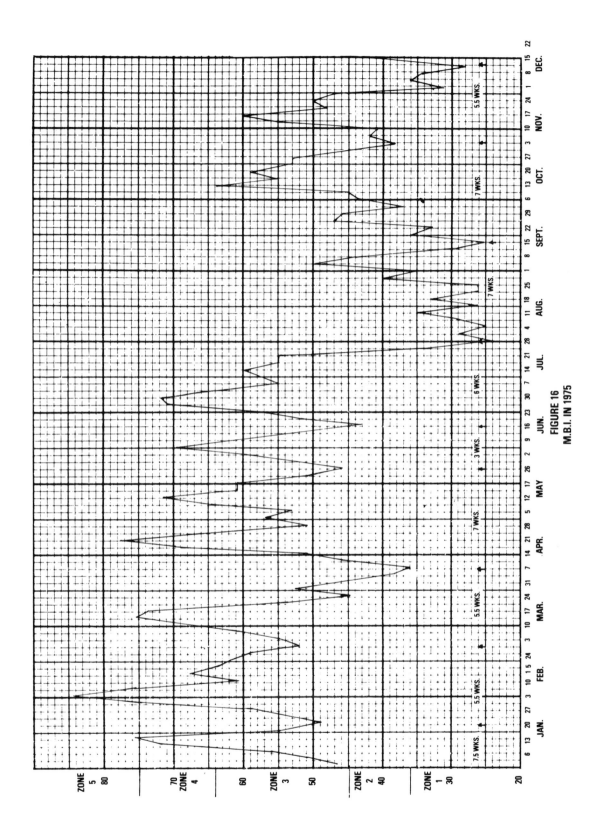

FIGURE 16
M.B.I. IN 1975

181

5) *Managing the position*

This is the most difficult part of the operation, but some clear ideas should have been formed at the time the map was made about the possible outcome. A realistic plan of evasive action is a must.

Let me give an example from 1974. It was one of my unsuccessful trades, but I did not make a bad situation worse by failing to take evasive action. I had a position in Merck against which I had written two calls. I was, however, not happy to note on 7/24/74, when the M.B.I. was 55, that Merck was still below its value from the last M.B.I. big-wave low (on July 10) and also was well below its value at the previous M.B.I. high when the reading was 55. (On 6/7/74 MRK was 83.7 when the M.B.I. was 54; on 7/24/74 MRK was 73.5 when the M.B.I. was 55). Therefore, I closed out the entire position, selling the stock and covering the options. My loss—$479. But that was the safest course of action as MRK promptly fell to 51. I could, of course, just have sold the stock and let the options fend for themselves or I could have sold more options. But I decided not to do this because it would tie up margin, which I planned to use elsewhere.

What I am really trying to get across is the necessity of examining the position in tune with the M.B.I. At what point should a profit be taken? We have already discussed Ed Thorp's play, shorting 3200 shares of Upjohn against the purchase of 50 calls. He initiated that position on June 11th. The June 10th M.B.I. reading was 51 (Zone 4)—so the short position was appropriate. Ed Thorp, of course, could not have known about the M.B.I. reading, but he is a smart man and I am sure has his own indicators. It is not exactly clear when the position was terminated. The Wall Street Journal just says "two weeks later." Let's take an exact two week period and go to Tuesday, June 25. The M.B.I. reading was 22 the previous day. Should profits have been taken there? Thorp apparently thought so, as he closed out the position and received $14,377 profit. Upjohn was then trading at 75.5 per share. It stayed around that figure as the M.B.I. bottomed out on July 11th and was still only at 76.2 at the next M.B.I. *high* on 7/25. We have just seen that failure to make it to a similar value at equivalent M.B.I. readings is bearish. So I believe the position could and should have been held from here until the next big-wave low on October 4th. The options would have expired worthless, but the stock had fallen to 45.5. If he had held on until 10/4/74, he would have lost $25,000 on the calls and gained $136,000!! on the short position, for a total profit of $111,000—almost 8 times what he actually received.

I have no experience of handling that kind of money, so I am not claiming that I would have done better than Thorp did. I am only pointing out the advantages of staying in tune with M.B.I. readings and how this indicator can be used as an intermediate timing device and how it can help in Portfolio Management.

6) *Tax Considerations*

Profit (loss) from option writing is treated as ordinary income gain (loss). You cannot treat it as capital gain (loss) and you cannot take capital gains (losses) against it. However, the situation is not necessarily unfavorable. Consider a 1:1 bearish spread that goes against one. The possible loss—(the strike spread less the basis) might be 3 points. Let us say the sell side shows a loss of 7 points and the buy side a gain of 4 points. The 7 points loss is deductible against ordinary income. So if you are in a 50% tax bracket, you save 3.5 points on income tax. And the 4 points is capital gain and can be set against (previous) capital loss. In other words, you break about even, and by judicious option writing it is possible to control the amount of ordinary income overall gain achieved in any tax year. Also, note the possibility of "rolling-over" options for an ordinary income loss in a rising market. Using this technique, option positions written at a lower strike are "brought-back" (for an ordinary income loss) and options of higher strike are sold. This gives upside protection and a genuine tax-deduction.

---

*The Clearing Corporation has been advised that, on March 2, 1976, a bill was introduced in the House of Representatives (H.R. 12224) which would change the tax treatment applicable to the writer of a call Option who engages in a closing transaction. The proposed legislation, if enacted into law, would tax gain or loss realized by a writer in a closing transaction as short-term capital gain or loss. The bill, as proposed, would apply to transactions which occur after March 1, 1976. In view of the uncertainty created by the proposed legislation, and pending congressional action thereon, investors should consult their own professional tax advisers regarding the implications of the proposed legislation.

CHAPTER 12

PUTS—
C.B.O.E. OPTIONS OF THE FUTURE?

Chapter 12

Puts—C.B.O.E. Options Of The Future?

There are many ways of achieving results. Certainly, the system herein described is not the only one that works; there must be many others. What the Moving Balance System offers is a logical way of working on either side of the market, for on any market day there will be buyers and sellers. Over the course of a short time, a useful idea can be obtained as to the direction of the market, and I believe that it is unduly restrictive to bet only on one side, the buy side, as so many "investors" do, when the sell side offers such promising rewards.

I do not fully understand why otherwise intelligent men really do not take the trouble to learn how to play the market properly. One hears an awful lot of nonsense talked. The nonsense itself is not that harmful because, after all, nobody really knows exactly where the market is going and nobody in the market is correct with the frequency usually demanded by one's non-market activities. But the nonsense inspires ideas like "It'll bounce back." "Just hang in there, you'll be all right." "Put it away in a drawer and forget about it." This is *suicidal*. Not only are there in the past staggering examples of fallen glory, but there will be more in the future. A friend of mine—a very competent physician practicing in a demanding surgical subspecialty—bought for his retirement plan (he belongs to a medical corporation) 200 shares of Polaroid at 140 = $28,000. I knew that he had done this as he told me that he had done so, one day back when Dow was talking to Jones. Casually, I asked him last fall if he still held his position in Polaroid. He looked at me as one might look at a talking frog—the

187

question was obviously absurd, "I bought that stock for my retirement," he said, thereby ending any further discussion. The talking frog said—"You bought at 140; the stock is now 20. How old do you think you will be when you can afford to retire?"

The trouble is that nobody entering the market feels there is much to learn (I certainly didn't). But the trouble also is that should anyone feel in need of help, it really *is* precious hard to come by. I had to read a lot of markedly *un*helpful books like *Why Most Investors Are Mostly Wrong Most Of The Time*, before finding anything of real value. Larry William's book helped me considerably. My system grew out of some of his ideas, as I have explained. But it grew in my way, not in his way, and it is my pleasure to describe it in the hope that it may be of use to others.

One of the beauties of simultaneous equations is that they can be seen to work. There is no argument. If the equation is right, everything falls into balance. So, hopefully, does my system. If a Zone 5 M.B.I. reading cannot be sustained and if, in its fall, the market falls with it, then money can assuredly be made on this observation alone.

But I do feel the lack of a good play for market lows in a bear market. As I mentioned previously, the premiums are not very favorable for a 1:1 bullish spread at big wave low reversals. Of course, in a really strong bull market the market itself will provide the support, but one badly needs a bullish play in a bearish market. And here is where *puts*, if the C.B.O.E. or Amex ever authorizes trading in them, will save the day.

What is a *"put?"*

A "put" is an option contract between buyer and seller. The seller (writer) of a put agrees to *buy from* the buyer of the put stock at *the strike price* during the life of the contract. I imagine that, if the C.B.O.E. gets into this field, a covered writer will be a player who is *short* the stock, whereas the naked writer will write the put against cash.

Let us examine the basic mechanics of the put.

Player A *sells* a put on stock ZYX presently trading at 50 per share and receives 6 per share.

Player B *buys* the same put for $600. It controls 100 shares of ZYX presently trading at 50 per share—what can happen?

1) *The stock declines to 30.*

Player B "puts" the stock to A who has to buy it from B for 50, the strike price.
Player B gains 50 – 30 – what he paid for the put (6) = 50 – 36 = *14* points.
Player A acquires stock for 50, the strike price, less 6, the put price received.
i.e., His 100 shares cost 50 – 6 = 44.
But they are only worth 30 in the open market.
The writer has lost *14* points.

But, just as there are covered and naked writers on the C.B.O.E. for calls, I am sure that if puts are traded there will be covered and naked put writers. Player A above is a naked writer. He has no protection nor can he acquire any by *owning* stock, as his contract is to *purchase* stock. But he can become a *covered writer* if he holds the stock *short* in his portfolio.

For instance, covered player C has the following position:

	Debit	Credit
Short 100 shares ZYX		5000
1 put 50 ZYX sold		600

ZYX falls to 30 and the stock is "put" to him at 50. His account will now look like this:

	Debit	Credit
Short 100 shares ZYX		5000
1 put 50 ZYX sold		600
100 shares ZYX bought (from exercise of put)	5000	

Obviously, he can liquidate his short position using the 100 shares he has acquired (when the put was exercised) and his profit will be 600 (less commissions).

2) *The stock rises to 70.*

The covered writer will begin to lose money as soon as the stock reaches 50 + 6 (the put premium required) = 56. He is in, basically, a similar position to the writer of a covered call when the stock *drops* below the price paid less premium received. The naked writer in this situation is golden as the put will lose value as the stock rises.

The *covered* writer at 70 will show the following position, if he covers:

	Debit	Credit
100 shares ZYX	7000	5000
1 put ZYX at 50		600

His loss is 7000 – 5600 = 14 points.

As with call writers, the writers of puts are at market risk, and as with call writers, the risks to writers of covered puts and naked puts will be on different sides of the market.

I am going to assume that if the C.B.O.E. gets into PUT options that it will do so in the same way that call options are presently traded. That is to say:

1) There will be no adjustment in strike price for dividends.
2) Jan., Apr., Jul., and Oct. options at fixed strikes will be traded. Also possibly Aug., Nov., Feb., May options.

If my assumptions prove to be correct at least two very interesting plays will be possible. Namely, *Play 14 Bullish Spread With Puts And Play 7 Multiple Put Spread.*

Play 14   Bullish Spread With Puts.

At a big wave low, put options would *acquire* value as stock prices drop. For instance, say there was a Jul *65* Upjohn *put* traded and the stock is presently at 50.2. Clearly such a put would have *intrinsic value* as the purchaser of the put could require the writer to buy stock from him at 65 when he, the purchaser of the put, could buy it in the open market for 50.2. It would have 65 – 50.2 = 14.8 points of *intrinsic value*, but it would also have a premium, as the market has been declining and presumably could go lower. The premium might be 4 points, so the put option would sell for 14.8 + 4.0 = *18.8* points. Similar thought processes apply to an Upjohn *50* put. This would be *all premium* and cost about 5. Here is the play:

AT A M.B.I. LOW

	Debit	Credit
Sell 1 UPJ 65 put		1880
Buy 1 UPJ 50 put	500	

The strike spread is 15. The basis is 13.8 (18.8 – 5.0 = 13.8). The maximum gain is at 65 or over when the basis (13.8) will be achieved, as both puts will be *worthless*. Remember, no one is going to put stock up for sale at any value under the market. The maximum possible loss is the strike spread minus the basis = 15.0 – 13.8 = *1.2*!! What a play!!

i.e., *stock falls to zero.*

At *zero* therefore, the Buy Side will show the following profit:

BUY SIDE

	Debit	Credit
50 option is worth 50	500	5000
Gain = <u>45 points</u>		

and the Sell Side will show the following loss:

SELL SIDE

	Debit	Credit
65 option is worth 65	6500	1880

Loss = <u>46.2 points</u>

Overall maximum loss = 1.2 points (SS – Basis).

Obviously, a more bullish spread could be arranged. Say 2 puts sold to one bought. Clearly, the maximum profit will be at 65 or above and downside breakeven point will be given by Formula 11.

Formula 11 Downside Breakeven Point "X" For Bullish Put Spread.

$$(LS - X) - A.P. = ((HS - X) - A.R.) \text{ No. of puts written.}$$

$$(50 - X) - 5 = ((65 - X) - 18.8) \, 2$$

$$(50 - X) - 5 = (130 - 2X) - 37.6$$

$$(50 - X) = (130 - 2X) - 32.6$$

$$32.6 = (130 - 2X) - (50 - X)$$

$$= 80 - X$$

Add X – 32.6 to each side

$$X = 80 - 32.6$$

$$= 47.4$$

At *47.4* therefore, the Sell Side will show the following profit (as each put is worth 17.6):

SELL SIDE

	Debit	Credit
Each 65 put is worth 65 – 47.4 = 17.6	3520	3760
	(17.6 x 2)	(18.8 x 2)
Profit = 2.4 points		

And the Buy Side the following loss:

BUY SIDE

	Debit	Credit
Each 50 put is worth 50 – 47.4 = 2.6	500	260
Loss = 2.4 points		

Below 47.4 the position will lose 1 point for every point lost on the common, because one put is unprotected.

Put premiums are often (in the over-the-counter market) somewhat less than call premiums, as investors are by and large bullish, but I feel some very safe bullish spreads with puts should be possible if the great day comes when they are traded on the C.B.O.E.

One interesting play—Play 7—A multiple put spread—involves the buying and selling of puts so any *change* is profitable. This play is as follows (let's consider the UPJ puts again).

SELL

	Debit	Credit
1 UPJ 65 put		1880
BUY		
3 UPJ 50 puts	1500 (5.0 x 3)	

The play is reminiscent of Thorp's play shorting 3200 shares of Upjohn and buying 50 calls, because what happens (assuming the stock is presently at 50.2), is that money is made if the stock goes up, money is made if the stock goes down—but there is a loss if the stock stays still. The stock at 50.2 is very close to the maximum loss point, the *lower strike*. What will the picture be there?

At *50* therefore, the Sell Side will show the following profit:

SELL SIDE

	Debit	Credit
Each 65 put now worth 15	1500	1880
Profit = <u>3.8 points</u>		

and the Buy Side the following loss:

BUY SIDE

	Debit	Credit
Each 50 put now worthless	1500	0
Loss = 15.0 points		
Overall loss (the maximum) = <u>11.2 points</u>		

What happens if the stock rises? Well, obviously at 65 both put options will be worthless and the possible profit will be the total amount received—TAR less total amount paid—TAP.

$$\text{Possible profit} = \text{TAR} - \text{TAP}$$
$$= 18.8 - 15.0$$
$$= 3.8 \text{ points}$$

The upside breakeven point (B) for Play 7 is clearly the higher strike less possible profit $= 65.0 - 3.8 = 61.2$.

At *61.2* therefore, the Sell Side will show the following profit:

SELL SIDE

	Debit	Credit
1 65 put would be worth 65 – 61.2 = 3.8	380	1880
Profit = <u>15 points</u>		

and the Buy Side the following loss:

BUY SIDE	Debit	Credit
3 50 puts worthless	1500	0
Loss = <u>15 points</u>		

There is also a downside breakeven point "X" at which the position *acquires* a profit as more puts were bought than sold. This point is given by Formula 12.

Formula 12 To Find "X" For Multiple Put Spread.

$$HS - X - AR = (LS - X - AP) \text{ No. of puts bought.}$$

$$
\begin{aligned}
65 - X - 18.8 &= (50 - X - 5) \, 3 \\
&= 150 - 3X - 15 \\
\\
46.2 - X &= 135 - 3X \\
2X &= 88.8 \\
X &= 44.4
\end{aligned}
$$

At *44.4* therefore, the Buy Side will show the following profit:

BUY SIDE

	Debit	Credit
Each 50 put is worth 50 − 44.4 = 5.6	1500	1680
	(5.0 x 3)	(5.6 x 3)
Profit = <u>1.8 points</u>		

and the Sell Side will show the following loss:

SELL SIDE

	Debit	Credit
Each 65 put is worth 65.0 − 44.4 = 20.6	2060	1880
Loss = <u>1.8 points</u>		

As I said, the position picks up profit from this point down as the stock drops, as there are more puts held than sold.

For instance, *with stock at 30* on expiration date:

BUY SIDE

	Debit	Credit
Each 50 put is worth 50 – 30 = 20	1500	6000
	(5 x 3)	(20 x 3)
Profit = <u>45 points</u>		

SELL SIDE

Each 65 put is worth 65 – 30 = 35	3500	1880
Loss = 16.2 points		
Overall profit 45 – 16.2 = <u>28.8 points</u>		

Notice that downside breakeven point was 44.4. 44.4 – 30 (the point studied) = 14.4.

We have just shown that at this point the overall profit is *28.8*, and this equals 14.4 x 2 = *28.8*. This is because there are two "unprotected" puts—the third balances the one sold.

The profit loss picture can be easily seen in Figure 17. This play will give a profit if the stock goes above 61.2 or below 44.4 on expiration date. These points are too far apart for real comfort, but the situation was chosen for illustration.

What other plays might there be?

1) *Straddles*
    A straddle consists of one call plus one put.

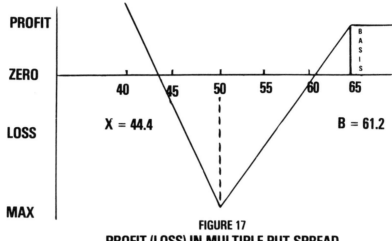

FIGURE 17
PROFIT (LOSS) IN MULTIPLE PUT SPREAD

2) *Straps*

A strap consists of two calls plus one put. Clearly this would be a high zone play with M.B.I. in Zone 4 or 5 (for the writer).

3) *Strips*

A strip consists of one call plus two puts. This would be a low zone play with M.B.I. in Zone 1 or 2.

These options exist already on over-the-counter option trading, but clearly if the C.B.O.E. traded puts we could go to all sorts of other combinations. What are the advantages and dangers of the basic straddle? There are, of course, straddle writers and straddle buyers. The writer of a straddle puts himself in danger of the option being exercised on both sides of the market, and though such a situation is unusual, he could get stock called from him (at a loss if he were naked), and then, if the stock dropped sufficiently, he could have the same stock put to him at a further loss. For these dangers he receives more premium than on a single option, but the advantage, I think, is really to the straddle buyer. If he buys a straddle on a volatile stock, he hopes to be able to make enough on one side of the straddle to yield him an overall profit.

Actually, I am not turned on by the straddle scene as one does not have enough control of the situation. But there will obviously be many opportunities for option trading in the future, even if the C.B.O.E. does not introduce put trading. The trading technique I now like best of all is spreading. A good spread set up in tune with the Moving Balance Indicator and as outlined previously is a very fine way to play the market via the C.B.O.E. and Amex. In order to make money, not only does money have to be risked, but also the risk of being incorrect in one's decision has to be faced. There is no great harm in being wrong, provided being wrong *activates protective mechanisms.* These prevent the loss of significant amounts of money, and since the successes should far outweigh the losses, there is nowhere to go but up. And that's a comforting feeling.

EPILOGUE

Epilogue

This is my system. It is a trading system based on the action of the market itself. Regular pull-backs occur even in a market in a sustained up-trend (such as the one from October 1962 to May 1965). Obviously, investment performance is improved by buying low and selling high. And since I have shown that the Moving Balance Indicator usually moves with the market, then I believe that it will be useful in the future when more violent swings in market action would seem to be likely.

The real value of the Moving Balance System is that it *is* a system, and that it will provide a feeling of self-confidence and a consistent and unemotional approach to decision making. *No longer will you feel at the mercy of the market, as you will be in balance with it.* So I wish you not luck, as luck is not part of the system, but perseverance; really to "map" out the plays; and patience, to wait until the M.B.I. has given the signal.

APPENDICES

Appendix I

The Three Levels Of The Volatility Index Are High, Medium, And Low.

Question	Vol. Index High	Medium	Low
1	a	c	b
2	c	b	a
3	a	b	c
4	c	a	b
5	b	c	a
6	a	b	c
7	c	a	b
8	c	b	a
9	c	b	a
10	a	b or c	b or c
11	b	c	a
12	c	a	b
13	a	b	c
14	b	c	a
15	b	c or a	a
16	a	b	c
17	a or c	c	b
18	b	c	a
19	c	d	a
20	c	b	a

In each column **circle** the answer you gave. Count 3 points for each answer in the High Volatility column, 2 points for each answer in the Medium Volatility column, and 1 point for each answer in the Low Volatility column. Derive your Volatility Index:

Maximum score 60
Minumum score 20
Any score over 45 = High Volatility
Any score below 30 = Low Volatility
Scores between 30 & 45 = Medium Volatility

Appendix II

Formulae

Symbols

B   = Upside breakeven point

X   = Downside breakeven point

AR   = Amount received per share
(stock and warrants—short,—option written)

TAR = Total number of points received

AP = Amount paid per share
(stock and warrants long—option bought)

TAP = Total number of points paid

EP = Exercise price (of warrants)

SPP = Stock price paid per share

SPR = Stock Price Received per share

WPR = Warrant price received per warrant

SP = Strike price (of options)

HS = Higher strike

LS = Lower strike

SS = Strike spread

OPR = Option price received

OPP = Option price paid

D   = B – HS

Mix   = No. warrants sold ÷ No. shares stock purchased

Formula 1   To find X in mix of stock long, warrants short
1 (pg 52)   X = SPP – (WPR) mix

Formula 2   To find B in mix of stock long, warrants short
2 (pg 53)   B – SPP = (B – (EP + WPR)) mix

Formula 3   To find B when stock long, options written
3 (pg 94)   B – SPP = (B – (SP + OPR)) No. of options written

Formula 4   To find B in unbalanced mix, stock short options bought
4 (pg 99)   (B – (SP + OPP)) No. options bought = (B – SPR) No.
                    shares sold ÷ 100

Formula 5   To find B for 1:1 bearish spreads
5 (pgs 111-112)   (AR –(B – LS) = AP

Formula 6   To find B in a multiple bearish spread
6 (pg 113)   (AR – (B – LS)) No. calls sold = (AP – (B – HS)) No. calls
                    bought

Formula 7   To find X in a 1:1 bullish spread
7 (pg 119)   X = LS + (AP – AR)

Formula 8   To find X in a multiple bullish spread
8 (pg 120)   (AP – (X – LS)) No. calls bought = (AR – (X – HS)) No.
                    calls sold

Formula 9   To find B in a multiple neutral spread
9 (pg 127)   B =HS + D
                    (D – AR) No. calls written
                        = (SS – AP + D) No. calls bought

Formula 10   To find B when B is below HS
10 (pg 158)   TAR – (B – LS) No. calls written = TAP

Formula 11   To find X for bullish put spread
11 (pg 192) $(LS - X) - AP = ((HS - X) - AR)$ No. puts written

Formula 12   To find X for multiple put spread
12 (pg 195) $HS - X - AR = (LS - X - AP)$ No. puts bought

Appendix III

Glossary

No. 1 Account—The cash account. All transactions are paid for in full. All securities held in this account are owned outright.

No. 2 Account—The margin account. Positions taken in a margin account are not owned outright as money has been borrowed from the brokerage house. The margin is the investor's percentage in the account.

No. 3 Account—The short account. This is a special subdivision of the margin used for recording securities held short. The equity in the account is kept at zero by the process of the mark to the market. Profit generated in the short account is transferred **to** the margin account. Loss necessitates transfer of money from the margin account, increasing the debit balance.

A/D Index—An indicator derived from two 10 day M.A.'s

$$\frac{10 \text{ day M.A. Advancing issues}}{10 \text{ day M.A. Declining issues}}$$

Advancing Issues—The total number of **issues** that advanced on any trading day.

Advancing Volume—The total number of **shares** that advanced on any trading day. The 10 day M.A. of the advancing volume is used in deriving the Moving Balance Indicator (M.B.I.).

Amex—The American Stock Exchange (also ASE).

Arbitrage—The practice of capturing the amount by which a convertible security is undervalued.

Average, 10 Day Moving—10 day M.A. derived by taking the 10 day total and dividing by 10. **Moving** refers to the process of adding the latest trading day and dropping the trading day 10 days previously.

Basis—The present (and variable) difference in price between a pair of options of different striking prices or expiration dates.

Bear—Someone who expects the market to go lower.

Big Board—The New York Stock Exchange (N.Y.S.E.). The M.B.I. is derived **solely** from figures relative to this exchange.

Bought In, To Be—The lender of certificates which have been sold short may at any time demand their return. Unless the broker can find another lender to furnish similar certificates, the short seller will be "bought-in" and his short position will be terminated.

Bull—Someone who expects the market to go higher.

Buy Side—The long side of a hedge or spread.

Buying Power—At the present initial margin rate of 50%, buying power is **twice the S.M.A.**

Buying Pressure—Part of Larry William's concept of market action.

B/S Index—

$$\frac{10 \text{ day M.A. \% buying pressure}}{10 \text{ day M.A. \% selling pressure}}$$

Call—A contract between call buyer and call seller.

Call Buyer—A player who acquires the right to buy stock from the call seller at a particular price—the strike price—at any time up to the expiration date.

Call Seller [Writer]—A player who contracts to deliver (sell) stock to the call buyer at a particular price up to the expiration date. He is a **covered** writer if he has a position in the underlying stock; a **naked** writer if he does not.

Commission—The broker's fee for carrying out your orders.

Cornering The Market—A player, or group of players, may achieve such control of a particular security that short-sellers are forced to pay excessive prices to cover. The play is illegal (see short-squeeze).

Cover, To—The closing out of a short position.

Covering Rally—A sharp run up in the price of a security is often attributed by brokers to significant short covering. I have never been able to find out if such is actually the case.

Debit Balance [D.B.]—The amount in a margin account borrowed from the broker. If no securities are held short, this figure does **not** vary with the market value of the position. However, the marking of the short account to the market **will affect** the debit balance.

Declining Issues—The total number of **issues** that declined on any trading day.

Declining Volume—The total number of **shares** that declined on any trading day.

Equity [Eq]—The player's money in a margin account. Equity (Eq) = market value of an account (MV) – debit balance (D.B.)

Excess Equity—The pleasant result of appreciation in the market value of a margin account. Excess equity—also called **S.M.A.**—is computed by taking the present equity of the account and subtracting 50% of the market value of the account.

Exercise Price—The price (of the common stock) at which a warrant becomes convertible into common stock.

Expiration Date—That date for both options and warrants on which the contract terminates.

Hedge—A play involving a security held on one side of the market balanced by a position in an option or warrant on the other side of the market.

House Call—Something physicians once made. Here, however, it means a house margin call.

Intrinsic Value—The actual amount (less commission) that would be received by exercising an option or warrant immediately.

Limit—Also called "stop." An order to buy or sell a security at a specified price. When a stop is triggered (on the Big Board), it becomes a market order, so the actual price paid or received may well differ from the stop price—and to the player's disadvantage of course.

Long Side Of The Market—The buy side. More than 95% of players use **only** the long side, to their great detriment in a down market.

M.A.P.—Market action plan. An essential step in the Moving Balance System.

Margin—The player's % equity in a margin account. **Initial** margin presently is at 50%—i.e., the player has to put up 50% of the money to initiate a position. **Maintenance** margin requirements vary with the brokerage house and are usually more than the 30% required by the N.Y.S.E.

Margin Account—A way of playing the market on margin. Securities are purchased with some of the player's money and some of the broker's money. The broker is safe as he keeps the certificates—in street name—as collateral against the loan. The player can gain (also lose) more on a percentage basis by playing the market on margin.

Margin Call—A reminder from the broker that stocks can depreciate in value and that this depreciation has declined to the level of the **maintenance margin**. The player can liquidate the position, or ante up more money to reduce the debit balance. If the house has requirements greater than those of the N.Y.S.E., the margin call will be a house call.

Market, At the—An order to the broker telling him in effect to buy (sell) securities immediately for the best price he can get. To put an order in "at the market" is naive in a skinny-dipping situation, but is acceptable in a hedge or spread when both sides will be undertaken in concert.

Market Value [M.V.]—The total market value of all the securities held in the No. 2 Account.

Mark To The Market—The No. 3 Account is marked to the market weekly in order to adjust the equity in the account to zero.

MKDS—What you punch on the Bunker-Ramo quote machine to get the Trader's Index.

MKDS—Assigned Value—A table for relating the 10 day M.A. MKDS positively to market action, as the MKDS itself is a reciprocal index. Used in calculating the M.B.I.

MKDS—10 Day M.A.—10 day M.A. of MKDS.

Moving Balance Indicator [M.B.I.]—Derived as follows:
    1) A/D x 10
    2) 10 day M.A. advancing volume ÷ 1000
    3) 10 day M.A. MKDS assigned value
    4) Total (1) (2) (3)
    5) Multiply by 2
       High values are over 60.
       Low values are below 21.

Moving Balance System [M.B.S.]—A system based on the M.B.I.

N.Y.Comp.—The New York Stock Exchange Composite Index.

OB—In golf it means out of bounds, but in the market it means "or better"—i.e., as part of an order to a broker. "sell 3 Jul **45's** for 6½ OB."

OTC—Over-the-counter—the third market.

Option—A contract between an option buyer and option seller. Options that have intrinsic value are said to be **in-the-money**. Those that are all premium are said to be **out-of-the-money**.

Overbought—Untoward buying and optimism.

Oversold—Untoward selling and pessimism.

PEA—Plan of evasive action. An essential ingredient in the game plan and a step in the M.A.P. Remember, nobody is correct all the time, so the PEA is your paddle when you are up the creek.

Play—A maneuver in the market.

Player—One who plays the market. He may call himself an investor if he does not know really what he is doing, or a speculator if he is prepared to go down in flames if he is wrong, or he may hire someone to play for him. But in the final analysis, the market is a **game** and all those in it are **players**.

Position—An opening transaction on either the long or short sides of the market.

Premium—The price a player is prepared to pay—over and above any intrinsic value—for acquiring rights to an option or warrant. It is also used to denote the total price paid for an option.

Prime Rate—The Federal Reserve Board fixes the rate at which member banks can borrow money. The banks in turn fix their prime (lending) rate; the rate at which their best (safest) customers can borrow money.

Put—A contract between put buyer and put seller.

Put Buyer—A player who acquires the right to put (sell) stock to the put seller at a particular price—the strike price—up to the expiration date.

Put Seller—A player who contracts to receive (buy) stock from the put buyer at the strike price at the expiration date.

Restricted Account—A margin account with margin below 50%.

Reversal, Big Wave—(see Zone concept).

Selling Short—A maneuver designed to generate profit as a stock declines. Short selling—or being short—is the most potent weapon available to combat a declining market. The really incredible thing is the lack of players on the short side. Of course, if you give your money to a money manager, he usually will not be allowed to sell anything short (though for the life of me I cannot understand why he is licensed to lose your money on one side on the market but not to risk it on the other hand). My private bet is that if every buy order you had made over the last few years could be changed to an order to sell short, and that the position could have been closed out in reverse, you would now be rather far ahead of the game.

Selling Pressure—Part of Larry William's concept of market action.

Short Side—The sell side of the market—that side that deals with short selling; or maneuvers, such as writing options, that aim to provide profit in, or at least protection against, a market decline.

Short-Squeeze—The process of getting caught in a corner.

Skinny-Dipping—Playing just one side of the market.

S.M.A.—Special Miscellaneous Account = excess equity.

Spread—A play using options (**not** stock) involving sell and buy sides.

Street Name—Margined securities are held in the name of the brokerhouse—street name—**not** in the name of the margin player. It's fair, as his share oftens ends up less than that of the house.

Straddle—A contract of one call plus one put.

Strap—A contract of two calls plus one put.

Strip—A contract of one call plus two puts.

Strike Price—The pre-arranged contract price for an option, effective during the life of the option.

Strike Spread—The difference between the striking prices of a pair of options. This figure does not vary.

Talking-Frog Syndrome—This disease affects many market "pros" when talking to those they consider amateurs. The "pros" are mutual fund managers, investment advisers, trustees, even those who manage their own pension funds. The sufferers from the disease have three characteristics:

1) Reluctance and, indeed, inability to listen to or discuss anything but "accepted" market theory.

2) The desire to establish superiority by the "you-are-a-talking-frog" look. The associated glassiness of eye is quite diagnostic. The look is effective at cowing the faint-hearted but **it has to be challenged.** Once I asked advice from a "pro" about warrant hedging. He said, "Well, it's all right, but you will have to watch it like a hawk." I replied, "But surely that's exactly what I **won't** have to do, as I will be hedged." The pro got a sudden attack of the talking-frog syndrome, tried cowing me with "the look," failed and then displayed the third characteristic.

3) Intense irritation. I really sympathize with the pro's because amateurs, after all, are "those who love" and their grasp of the subject they love should obviously be far below that of the professional who spends his whole time at it. If I were a fund manager and someone named Lloyd, a pathologist for heaven's sake, said, "I **know** I can do far better for myself than you could do in your fund" and further "You are playing the market all wrong, " I know **I** would get a bad case of the talking-frog syndrome.

Trader's Index = MKDS

$$= \frac{\dfrac{\text{No. advancing issues}}{\text{No. declining issues}}}{\dfrac{\text{advancing volume}}{\text{declining volume}}}$$

Uptick—A rule for shorting a stock or warrant designed to maintain an orderly market.

V.I.—The Volatility Index.

Warrant—A contract issued by a corporation guaranteeing convertibility of the warrant into a pre-arranged number of shares of common stock at a pre-arranged price of the common stock (exercise price) at any time up to the expiration date.

Writer—One who sells an option contract. He is either a **covered** writer if he holds a position in the underlying stock or a **naked** writer if he does not.

Zone Concept—This is based on the M.B.I. and holds that the market **on any trading day** can be put into one of five zones:
Zone 5: Up—absolutely primed to go down = big wave reversal imminent.
Zone 4: Up—intermediate high (and possible small wave reversal).
Zone 3: The normal trading range.
Zone 2: Down—intermediate low (and possible small wave reversal).
Zone 1: Down—absolutely primed to go up = big wave reversal imminent.

Appendix IV

Selected Bibliography

Ansbacher, M.G., **The New Options Market**, Walker and Company, 720 Fifth Avenue, New York, N.Y., 10019, 1975.
This book contains much sound advice, but the author has the philosophy that it is impossible for anyone to predict with accuracy the price movement of a stock, at least during the short time-span of its options.

Appel, G., **Winning Market Systems**, 2nd Edition, Signalert Corp., Distributed by Windsor Books, 1974.
An excellent book full of information on stock market systems.

Appel G., **Double Your Money Every Three Years**, Windsor Books, P.O. Box 280, Brightwaters, N.Y., 11718, 1974.
All sorts of money-making plays, including a chapter on options.

Clasing, H. K., Jr., **The Dow Jones-Irwin Guide To Put And Call Options,** Dow Jones-Irwin, Homewood, Illinois, 60430, 1975.
Various strategies in terms of their risk to reward ratio are examined. C.B.O.E. analogs to the standard warrant diagram are given, with guidelines for strategy in terms of stock price and option premium.

Gastineau, G. L., **The Stock Options Manual,** McGraw Hill Book Company, 1975.
This book gives full coverage of all aspects of option trading except market timing. Gastineau concentrates on trying to find the fair value of an option as derived from various models. Overvalued options are sold; undervalued options are bought. This book has a fine bibliography.

Gross, L., **The Stockbroker's Guide To Put And Call Option Strategies,** New York Institute of Finance, 2 New York Plaza, New York, N. Y., 10004, 1974.
A lucid account of the over-the-counter option market, as well as the Chicago Board of Options Exchange.

Hurst, J. M., **The Profit Magic Of Stock Transaction Timing**, Prentice-Hall

Inc., Englewood Cliffs, New Jersey, 1970.

The only time I tried this system I got creamed, but I think that some interesting results should be possible using it in combination with the Moving Balance System.

Lloyd, H.E.D., **Spread Trading In Listed Options**, Humphrey E. D. Lloyd, M.D., 23 Pearl Street Extension, Beverly, Ma., 01915, 1976.

20 spreads with calls; 5 with puts are described. The advantages and disadvantages of each spread, as well as the position it occupies on the Option Grid, are described.

McMillan, L. G., **How To Make Money With Stock Options,** Exposition Press, Hicksville, New York, 1975.

This book is a short survey of option trading.

Miller, J. T., **The Long And The Short Of Hedging,** Henry Regnery Co., 180 No. Michigan Avenue, Chicago, Illinois, 60601, 1973.

Deals mainly with warrant hedging. Useful section on margin accounts and regulation T (12 CFR 220)—credit by brokers and dealers—is given in full.

Miller, J. T., **Options Trading,** Henry Regnery Co., 180 No. Michigan Avenue, Chicago, Illinois, 60601, 1975.

Noddings, T. C., **The Dow Jones-Irwin Guide To Convertible Securities**, Dow Jones-Irwin, Homewood, Illinois, 60430, 1973.

An excellent book for the serious and patient investor who wishes to hedge using convertible securities.

Noddings, T. C., Zazove, E., **C.B.O.E. Call Options: Your Daily Guide To Portfolio Strategy**, Dow Jones-Irwin, Homewood, Illinois, 60430, 1975.

This expensive book presents, in loose-leaf format, valuable exhibits for assessing over—or under—valuation of listed options. Four updates are included in the price.

Platnick, K. B., **The Option Game**, CommuniConcepts, 119 W. 57th Street, New York, N. Y., 10019, 1975.

The approach is basic, the style at times staccato.

Thomas, C. W., **Hedgemanship: How To Make Money In Bear Markets, Bull Markets, And Chicken Markets While Confounding Professional Money Managers And Attracting A Better Class Of Women**, Dow Jones-Irwin, Homewood, Illinois, 60430, 1970.
After all that, the book is a superficial examination of hedging and hedge funds, with a small section on options.

Thorp, E. O., Kassouf, S. T., **Beat The Market,** Random House, New York, N. Y., 1967.
The first book to examine warrant hedging scientifically. A very important book in helping anyone understand short selling, and hedging.

Williams, L. R., **The Secret Of Selecting Stocks For Immediate And Substantial Gains**, Conceptual Management, Carmel Valley, California, 1972.
I have indicated in the text the important part this book played in the development of the Moving Balance System.